MW00749124

Also by Ori Hofmekler

Hofmekler's People

HOFMEKLER'S GALLERY

ORI HOFMEKLER

HOFMEKLER'S GALLERY

FOREWORD BY MARTIN PERETZ

Times BOOKS

Published in the United States by Times Books, a division of Random House, Inc., New York, and simultaneously in Canada by Random House of Canada Limited, Toronto.

Thirty-eight of the caricatures in this book were previously published in *Penthouse*. One appeared on the cover of *The New Republic*.

Library of Congress Cataloging-in-Publication Data
Hofmekler, Ori, 1952–
Hofmekler's gallery.
1. Biography—20th century—Caricatures and cartoons.
2. Celebrities—Caricatures and cartoons.
3. Israeli wit and humor, Pictorial. I. Title.
CT109.H64 1987 920'.009'09 86-23122
ISBN 0-8129-1596-8 (pbk.)

Manufactured in the United States of America
9 8 7 6 5 4 3 2
First Edition

Book Design: Jessica Shatan

FOR DANIEL AND SHIRA

ACKNOWLEDGMENTS

I want to thank Bob Guccione, for the freedom he has given me to use my imagination and for his help and cooperation, and Jonathan Segal, who helped develop this project from the first idea to the finished book.

FOREWORD

BY MARTIN PERETZ

The painting on the cover of this book—Lee Iacocca as Bruce Springsteen—like so many of Ori Hofmekler's images is not obvious comment.
But it is acute comment. And it certainly must have made both of its sub-
jects writhe just a little. Of course it also makes us laugh—and laugh precisely because of its startling and penetrating accuracy. It is part of Ori
Hofmekler's special gift, abundantly on display in the pages that follow,
that he can rearrange our perceptions of public people we think we
already know. Once he has revealed them to us—or undressed them—they
cannot in fact be the same again. Sometimes Hofmekler's revelations pro-
voke deep belly laughs, sometimes wry laughter only to oneself. But the
damage has been done. It is the kind of wonderfully mischievous damage
for which we now revere Honoré Daumier.

Daumier's work offers us a nearly comprehensive, if not exactly system-
atic, depiction of the social and psychological character of nineteenth-
century France. Daumier left in pen, paint and print a daily record of his
commentary—often five or six commentaries on the moral incongruity or
discordance of the moment. Taken together, the little conceits and grand
pretensions that provoked Daumier are the inner history of classes and
nations in their unguarded, sometimes even intimate and also public representations.

The artist as satirist and observer is not of course a phenomenon dating
only to the last century. Hieronymus Bosch's great canvas *The Bearing of
the Cross* (1505), on which is assembled a nightmarish parade of hateful
faces, none of them directed toward the Messiah of love, is just one
instance of the tradition exposing the portentous hypocrisy of the pious.

When authority shifted in the eighteenth century from high clergy to the
secular priesthoods of power and money, the targets also shifted. Caricature, from the Italian for loading, is how it was done and is done to this
day. But with a difference. Simply overloading features or physiognomy,
however inventively, would no longer suffice either to illumine some elu-

sive point of individual or group personality or even to entertain. What Daumier did was to flesh out the visual character of social cohorts, large or small, already recognizable or just then emerging as acknowledged actors (often only grudgingly acknowledged) in the theater of modern life.

In America, we no longer tend to see distinct social groups and classes. We are all, rich and poor, influential and nameless, soulful and oblivious, clad body and spirit in designer jeans. While Daumier saw through the collective disguises of mug and garb, he also depicted those who sat in the seats of the mighty so mercilessly that a century and a half later we still see Louis Philippe, for example, as he did. But Daumier's special genius, like that of George Grosz, was the personalized face of the mass. We are now back, in our visual satire, to the depersonalized face of the individual and of the individual politician in particular.

Take Richard M. Nixon. The pivot of his face is his long nose, an inevitable suggestion of Pinocchio, the liar. A superficial analogy at best. Nixon, though, was not just a sneak, not even primarily that. But even someone so alert and skilled as David Levine didn't get much beyond the self-evident nose and its no less self-evident meaning. Over the generation in which Nixon seemed to haunt our national life, there were cruel representations of him, but none that I recall actually located him in the nervous mobility and desperate insecurity from which, even at the pinnacle, he could not escape. Daumier saw, however, a thousand times, the vulnerabilities not only of historical individuals but of lawyers, doctors, bankers, wives. It is why Daumier is both great artist and historian.

I do not want to make extravagant claims for Ori Hofmekler, an Israeli artist trained and self-trained in the classical tradition. But he is rare in that he does not separate his high or fine art from the ostensibly lower art of social and political observation. Here Hofmekler is precisely like Daumier; and in the elusive fluidity of his paint, and especially in his watercolors, we cannot but be reminded of some of the masters. Hofmekler is thirty-four years old, too early still to be sure what openings (or closures) there might yet appear in his career. He has not found or even searched his way to social types as his topic. But the Israel from which he comes and the neighborhood in which its people live presented him with a rogues' gallery of extreme personalities, an invitation to caricature not just of feature but of character. This he does without peer.

So why does he not appear regularly in the mainstream or prestige periodical press? Well, actually, outside America he does. Paradoxically, more traditional societies seem less inhibited and constrained than our own about what is visually permissible by way of comment on character. And in the modern world, the exploration of character leads inexorably into the dark corners, not necessarily of private sexual behavior but almost certainly of the sexual metaphor in public life. "Hofmekler's People," as his monthly feature is called, appears regularly in *Penthouse*, where the sexual metaphor does not jar—though where it is probably often misunderstood. The less laden illustrations find their way into the weekly newsmagazines and into other publications like my own *New Republic*. But Hofmekler deserves not only a large audience (which he gets from *Penthouse* publisher Bob Guccione) but a regular one in the opinion elites. And not only because he is exceedingly good pictorially. He deserves it because his work is often a unique expression of the psychology behind today's headlines.

I do not know precisely what Ori's own political biases are. What is clear is that he has a terrible allergy to political cant, which is sometimes mistaken for heavy thinking. There is also the discomforting irony that he sometimes makes strong comment on a particular personality and that opponents of that personality think his image a ready political weapon. It does not always work. Take, for example, the pinkish Margaret Thatcher as the roller derby queen whose most prominent feature is her balls. I know literally dozens of people who thought the image devastating. I think it is a little *homage*, in the French sense. Which side is Hofmekler on?

One image that particularly offended people was the Ayatollah Khomeini on the can (actually an oil barrel). A holy man, no less. This actually was a literary or, more properly, literate allusion. Khomeini's theological writings are fixed on the cloacal dimension in life. This mullah's world view is, then, truly holistic. No one made this clearer than Hofmekler. He is alarmed by the increasing sway religious fanatics hold over our lives. It is a part of his experience as an Israeli . . . and also as someone who has lived and worked in America. The sexual metaphor is easily suggested by the sexual obsessions of our "moral majority." Not since James Agee's screenplay *The Night of the Hunter* and possibly not since Sinclair Lewis's *Elmer Gantry* have we had more vivid insight into the psychic world of the divinely inspired hustler. In several striking pieces, Hofmekler explores the animating ambivalences of such figures as Jerry Falwell and Jimmy Swaggart, showing that in a culture where sexuality often means money, lots of it, so does the fear of sexuality. As he presents these big-time TV men of God, they are both powerful and pathetic, covering their shame with the fig leaf of moral certainty.

Was it moral certainty or political calculation that persuaded even someone so irreverent as New York's Mayor Ed Koch to remove from the city's public billboards Hofmekler's poster of the slim-fingered hands of the women's movement grasping to crunch Fritz Mondale's crotch? In this vignette of the Democratic party's captivity, its inability even to consider a male as a candidate for vice president, Hofmekler grasped the entire debacle of 1984. It was the smartest remark I saw on the election.

Ronald Reagan is one of the lead players in Ori Hofmekler's dramatis personae on the big stage of contemporary politics. He understands deeply one of the secrets of that politics, which is that, outside the communist orbit and the Third World, it does not impose itself by raw self-assertion. It does so by submerging the politicians' own characters in that of the culture heroes and styles of society. Hofmekler's Reagan-as-Rambo may be the (and his) most direct portrayal of how the president often does not or cannot distinguish between celluloid memory and the real and risky possibilities of power. I am convinced Hofmekler understands the Rambo fantasy or other dreams of glory, honor, even retribution; that he grasps the complexity of how such ambitious psychic consolations are perilous but also how, without them, life and politics would not necessarily be more safe or more sane. But then this book is to allow you to judge for yourself.

For some time now I have been conscious of the fact that I sell paintings of politicians and other celebrities in just about the same way Donald Duck and Mickey Mouse images are sold. I, too, am creating images I hope will be commercially successful in the marketplace. But unlike those wonderfully well-established Disney stars, I feel the pressure of the moment. We live in a time of rapidly passing fads: what is hot and what is not makes an enormous difference. And that changes so quickly, and there are so many "products" competing for the public's attention.

But I don't want to be controlled by daily events; they are too misleading. Often only when the dust has settled am I able to see the true significance of events. My intention therefore is not to be a daily cartoonist. As a result I sometimes deal with a figure that was "hot" a while back. And yet ironically my paintings can predate real events—"Schwarzenegger Commando" was done before President Reagan initiated his now-famous attack on Libya; my "Rambo" piece was painted before Sylvester Stallone was invited to the White House.

Perhaps that is because I try to get to the essence of a particular point of view, to ignore immediate reactions and overreactions to a single event (again, this is why I'll follow a figure for quite a while before I paint him). Seen with some perspective, it becomes clear that many issues or events are the same anyway, that they are just happening over and over again in a new place, in a new way, involving different characters. If there is something wrong with the way the CIA does things, for instance, you'll see it manifesting itself time and time again, be it in Chile, Indochina, El Salvador, Nicaragua.

Politics is sold like any other product on the market. Political theories are based on the "good" and the "bad" in society's conscience just like television films and soap operas reflect society's values. But through the media's dominance of people's lives, all the aspects of our lives overlap. People belong to a political camp in the same way they identify with a sports team. But though politics is all around us, it is a difficult subject to deal with artistically. And what I find myself doing is not trying to clarify political statements—I am not at all political myself—but to present political figures in a different context, to expand on words and actions.

In my own mind, I attempt to create what I call "the show." Which explains, I suppose, why I have tried to use visual imagery from the entertainment world, the world of art, and consumer products (those wonderful ads and commercials!) in which to portray the central figures of my painting. More and more it seems the boundaries between those worlds are blurring anyway. One thing is certain: for the show I want to put on, peopled with larger than life characters, I need powerful settings—a Hitchcock film, a Botticelli painting, a famous brand of scotch.

Because my approach is somewhat different from the standard, I sometimes feel like a theater director who has chosen to stage a well-known play and then introduced images or characters from a different world—a process akin to auditioning actors before they see the script. So very often I need to use live models and costumes to complete a scene. A man with physical dimensions resembling Andrei Gromyko's will pose like the principal figure in the film *The Woman in Red*. Or I'll use a woman who resembles Margaret Thatcher in approximate size, or a man whose baldness is similar to Ed Koch's. That helps keep my feet on the ground.

And whether it is politics, real life or art, I find myself inevitably choosing between good and bad. The only problem is that in my work in the political arena I find myself more and more having to invent the good guys, and of course neither side fits squarely in a category.

I graduated from the Bezazel Academy of Art in Jerusalem with romantic dreams about my future as an artist. Although I had prepared myself for it, the fall into real life from the academic Olympus was traumatic. Was I just drawing to decorate walls or was I drawing the world I lived in? The real world was a challenge to me in a peculiar kind of way. In Israel, the morning paper and the news reports about the politics of the day seemed at the time to be the height of the banal, mired in ideology, rigidity, absolutes, self-fulfilling prophecies. And yet I believed then that the more idiotic, dumb and trite the subject matter, the more it could be of interest. Now, working from the United States, in the middle of a career as a political artist, I find it is the complexity that interests me, the conflict.

Politics oversimplifies life. Every establishment has rules, and people will identify with you if you, as a ruler, appear good enough, and if you identify for them what is clearly bad. Every good guy needs a bad guy to attack. In my work now I try to put back into the equation whatever the good guy has identified as anathema, the thing that will shake up the world for him. For the communists, it is capitalism; for America, it is communism; for fundamentalists, it is sex and rock 'n' roll. All of these groups make the mistake of seeing the world as very simple indeed. Events are put in easily defined categories. For me as an artist, I see all of that as kitsch—an attempt to create simplistic categories for a world that in actuality is built on absurdities. Kitsch is an attempt to erase the question marks attached to daily events, giving people simplistic information. This black and white definition of good and bad is at the root of politics, and I deeply fear it. The man who will finally press the button to begin a nuclear war will be the man who believes in a world that is divided rigidly and simply into the good and the bad.

Satire was intended to attack this vision of the world. After all, a good joke is often about a taboo. But when I hear the news, it often sounds like a satire, and I ask myself, is it satire or is it real life? I suppose one could ask me the same question about my work.

—Ori Hofmekler
New York
December 1986

HOFMEKLER'S GALLERY

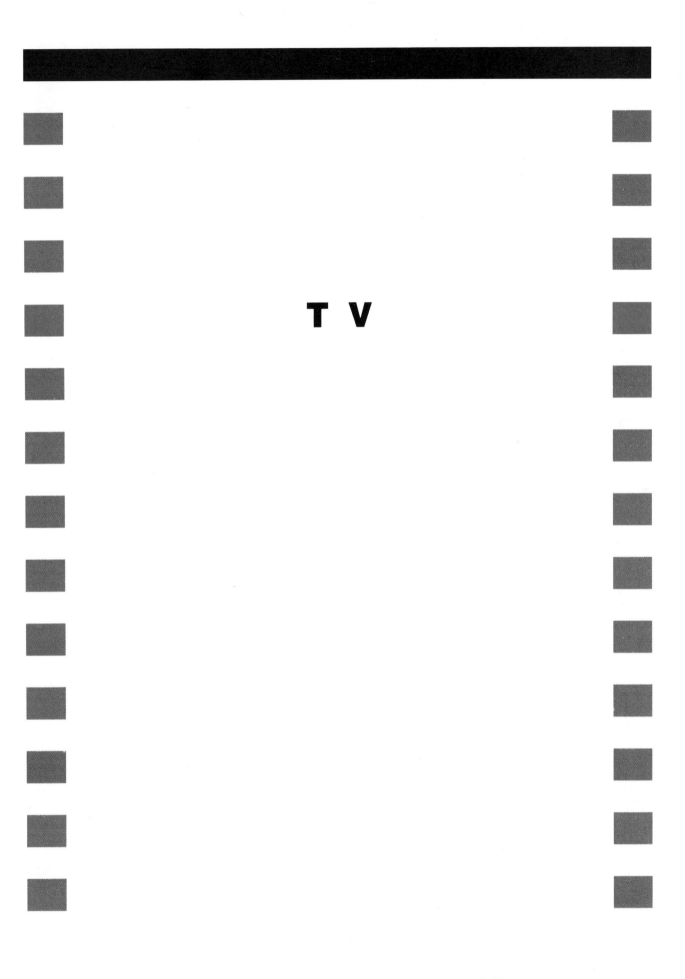

TV

M*A*S*H

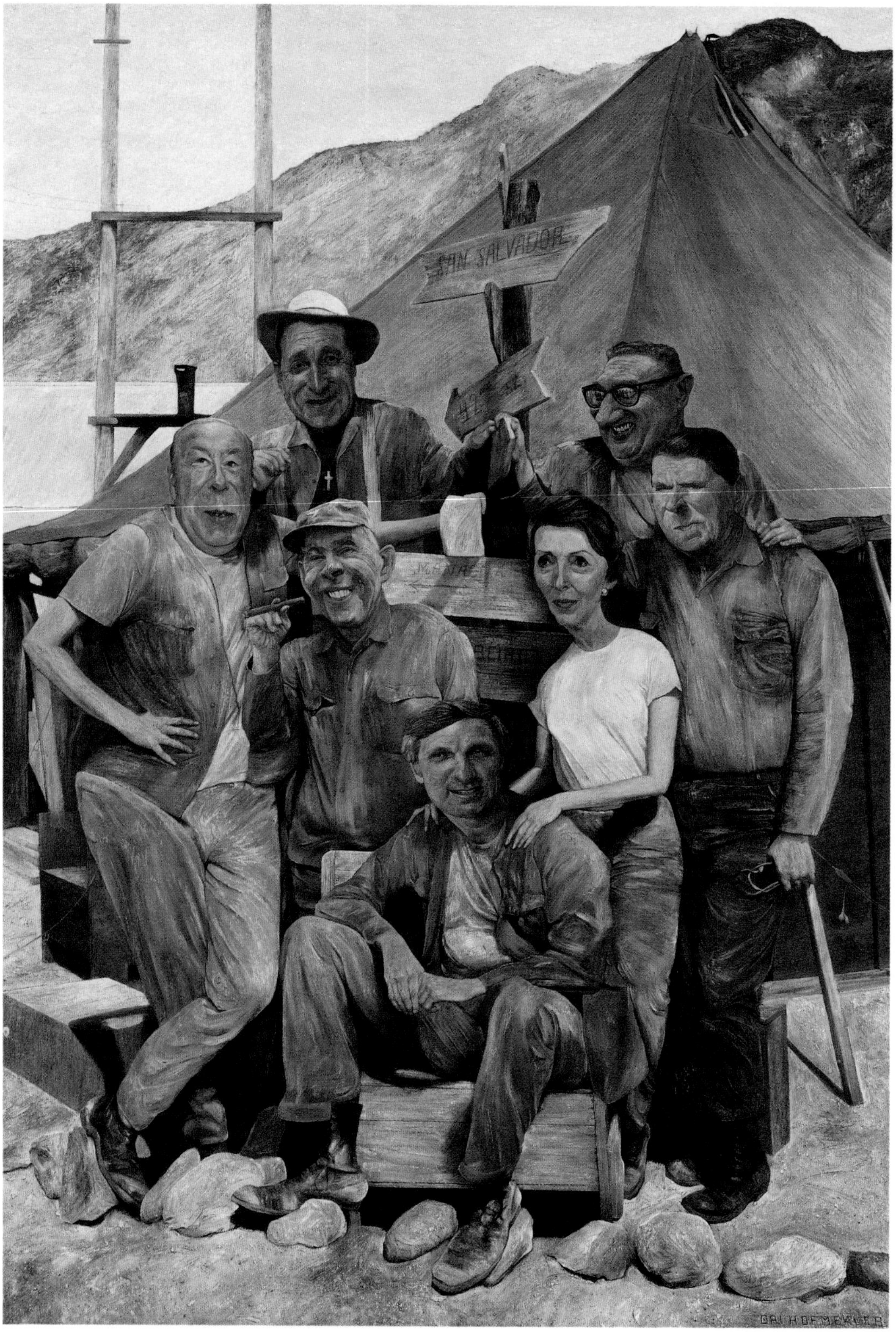
SAN SALVADOR
ORI HOFMEKLER

PRESIDENT OF THE UNITED STATES RONALD REAGAN AND HIS ADVISERS

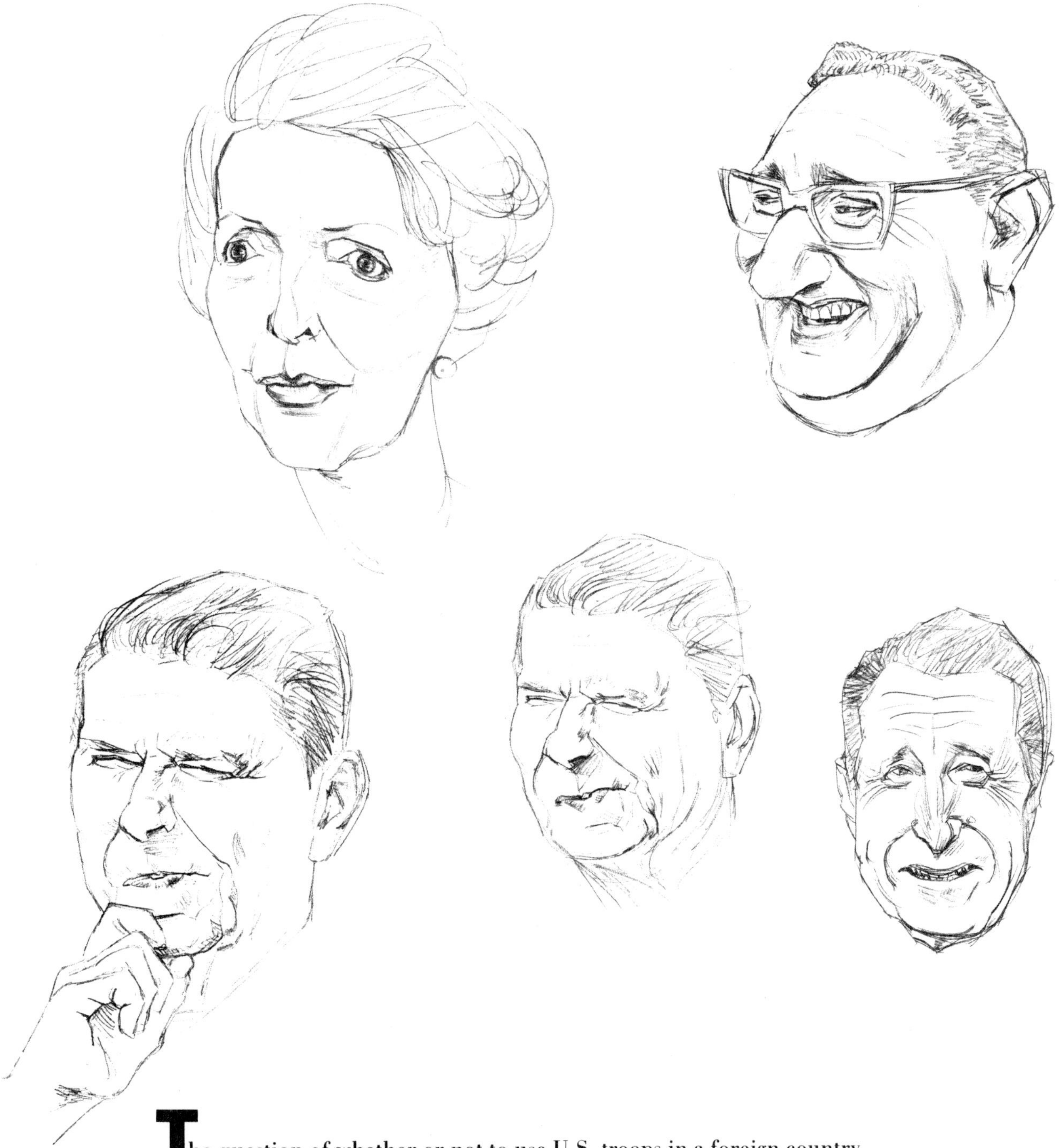

The question of whether or not to use U.S. troops in a foreign country has always been controversial. This piece was done when U.S. involvement in Central America was a major issue. The TV series *M*A*S*H* was about to end. I liked the show—especially its realism—and I know Reagan likes to play war games with a lot of cameras and media around. I guess he wants history to remember him as the greatest leader of the American nation.

Nancy is taking the feminine role—what else. I left Captain Benjamin Franklin Pierce (Alan Alda) and Colonel Sherman Potter (Harry Morgan) from the TV series to emphasize that Reagan is always just part of a show. When I say "a show," I mean that he plays to the cameras, he has almost an absurd theatricality, as if he were still making those B movies. In many ways I would prefer to see the president and his bunch on a TV series than in real life.

BUCKINGHAM DALLAS

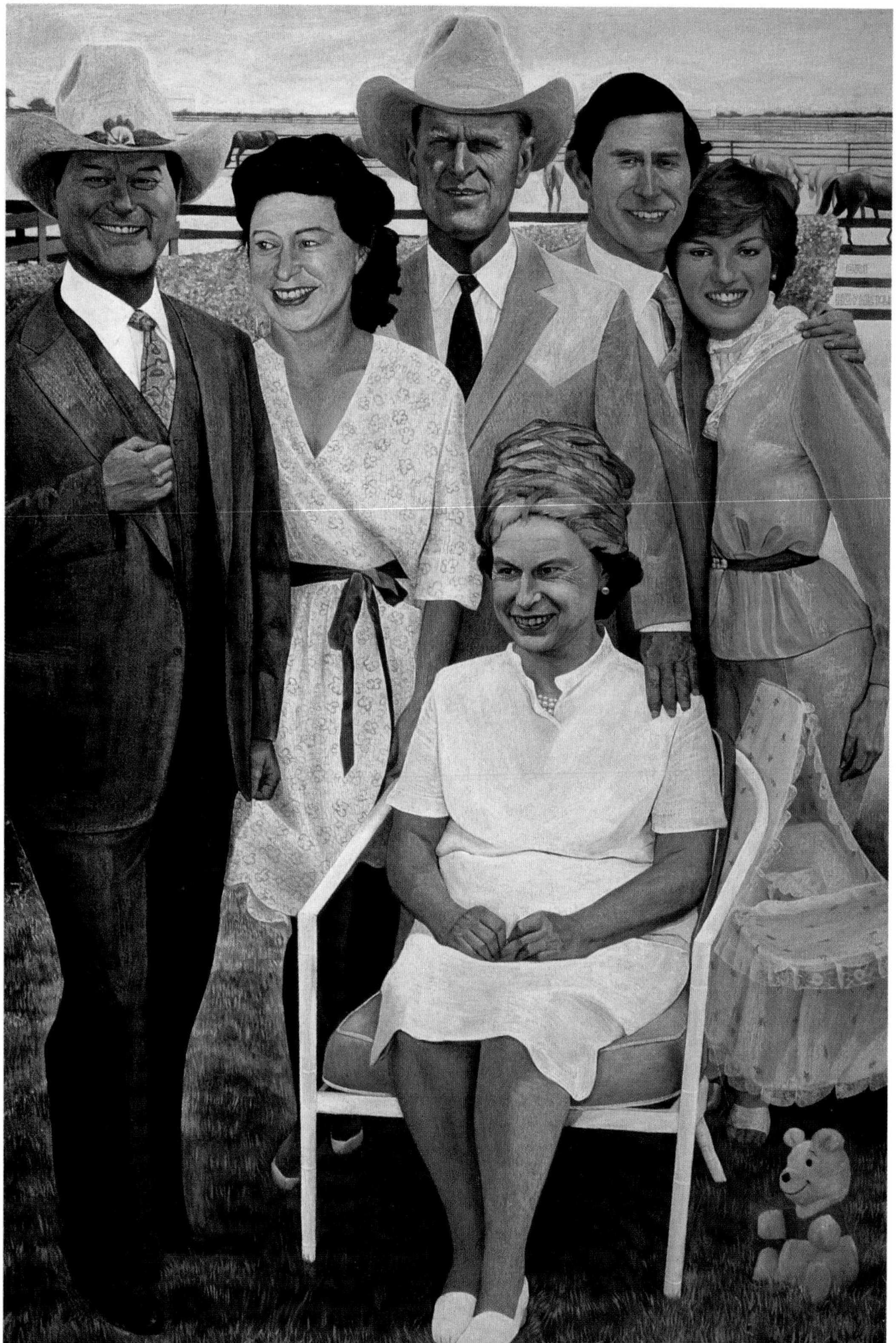

THE ROYAL FAMILY

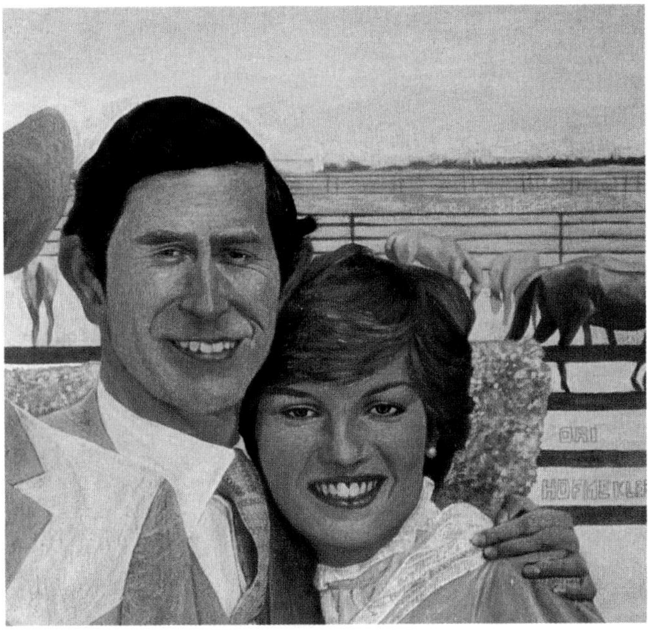

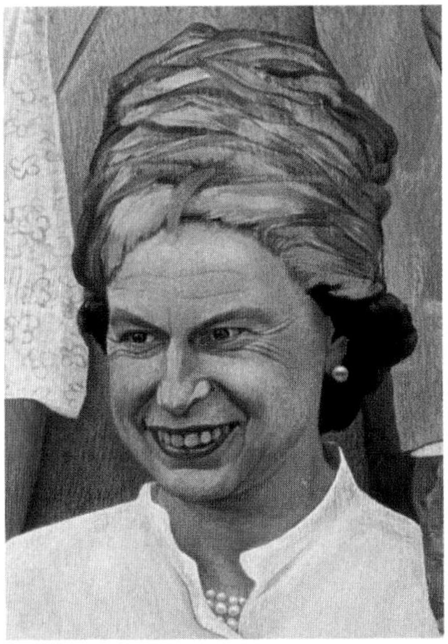

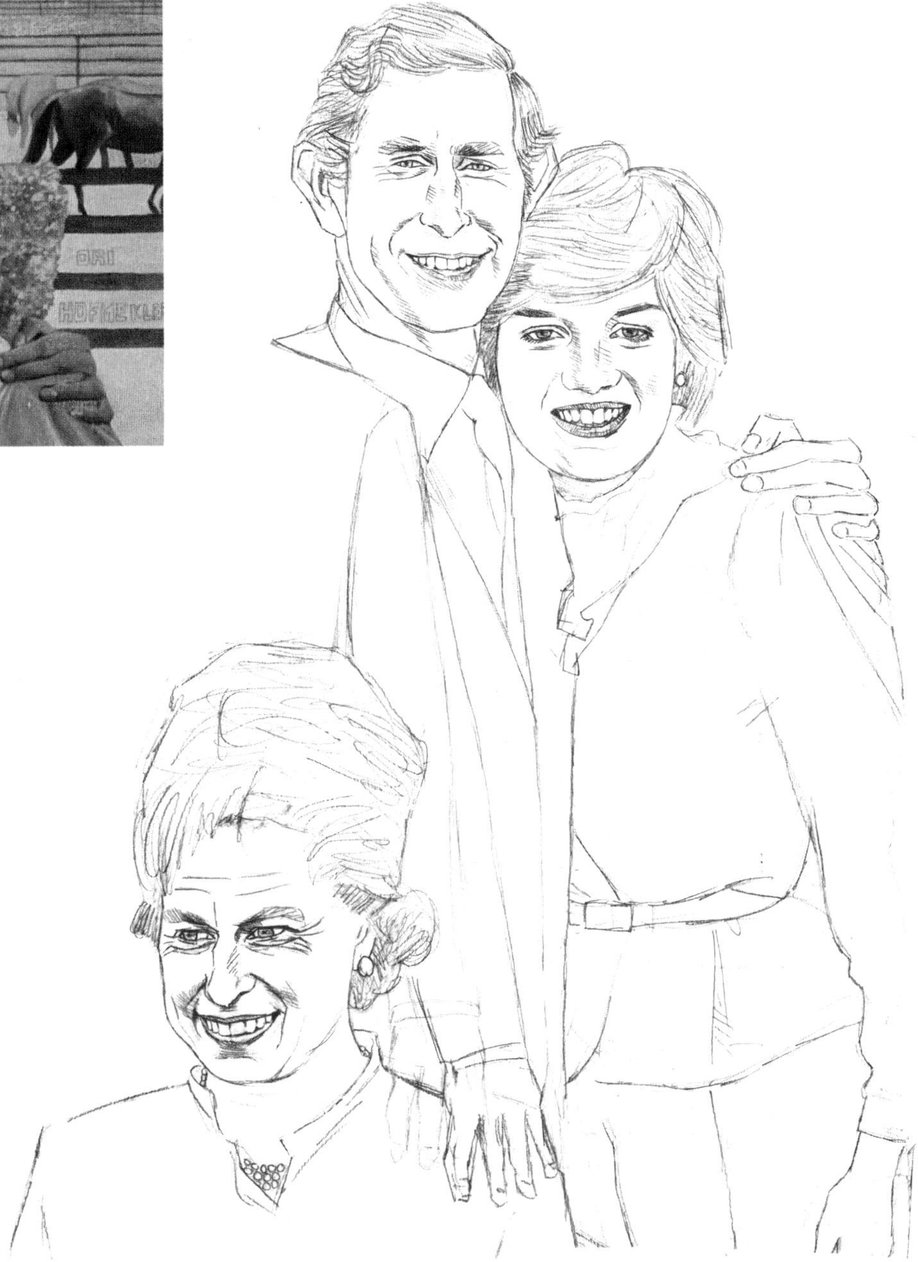

I like to think that Buckingham Dallas could easily replace *Dallas.* The Queen could take the place of Miss Ellie. The Duke could take the role of the patriarchal father, Jock Ewing. Diana could switch easily with sexy Pamela, and Prince Charles would then be husband Bobby.

Bobby is a nice guy—good for Charles.

The only problem here was the bad guy. I had to leave Larry Hagman in the scene as J.R. because without him how can we really differentiate between the good guys and the bad guys?

MR. T.

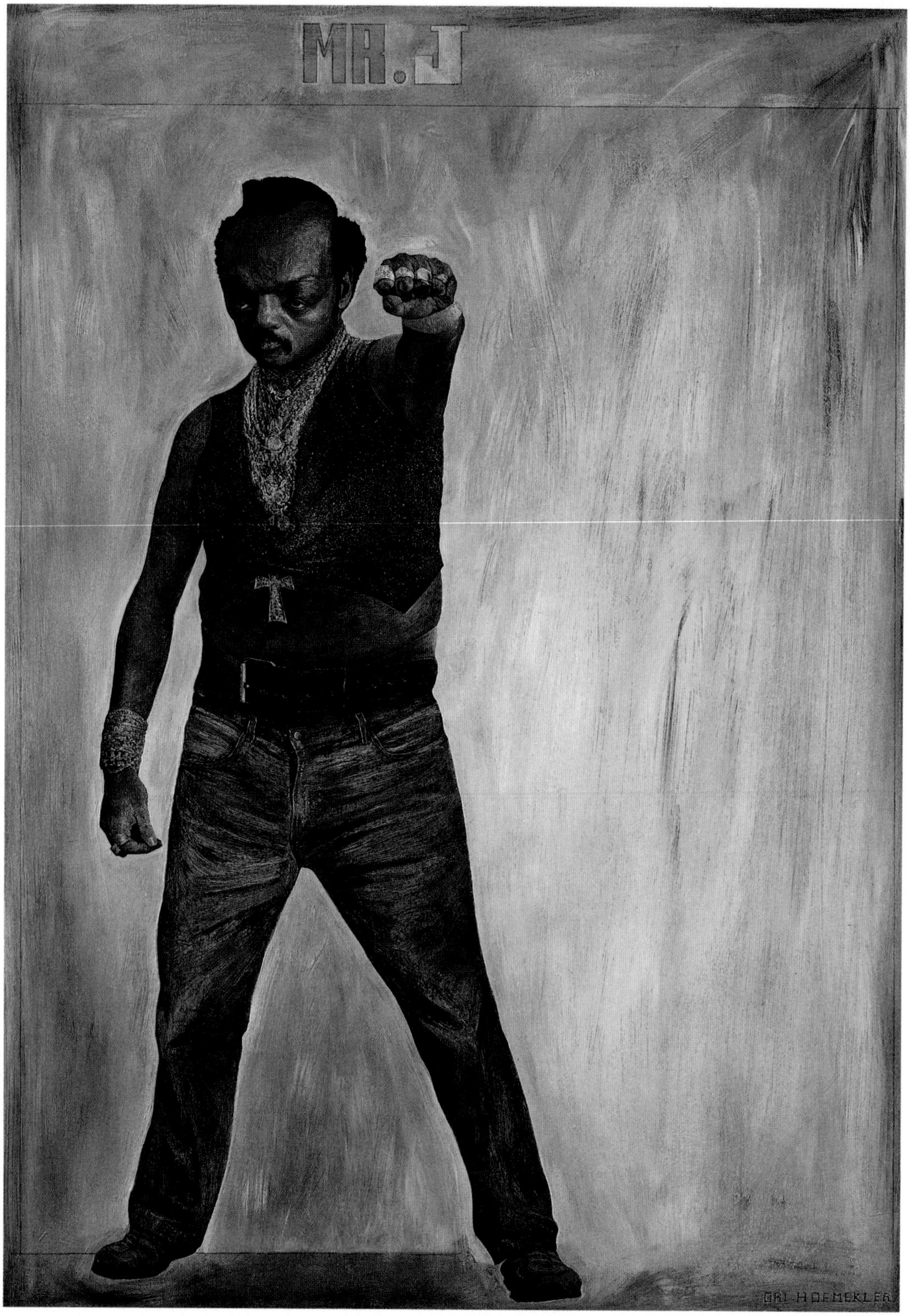
MR. J
ORI HOFMEKLER

REV. JESSE JACKSON, FOUNDER AND EXECUTIVE
DIRECTOR OF OPERATION PUSH,
FORMER PRESIDENTIAL CANDIDATE

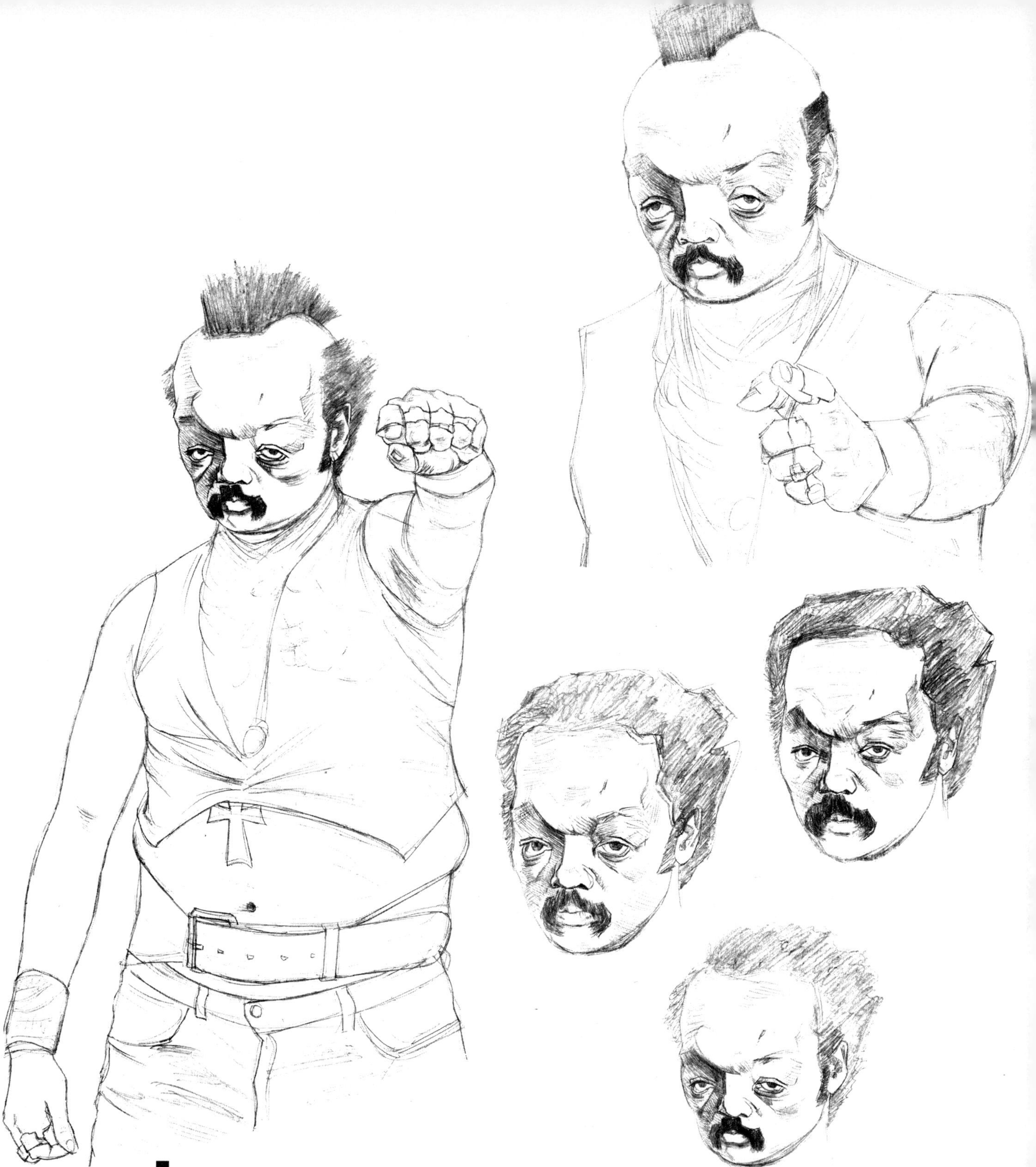

If the Democratic leaders were *The A-Team*, Jackson would definitely take the role of Mr. T. But since the Democrats are far less united I figured I had to give Jesse a solo.

Like Philip Michael Thomas on *Miami Vice*, Mr. T is what I call the black balance. Jesse Jackson has the same role for the Democrats in the political show.

I like Mr. T. America loves him. Nancy Reagan loves him. Good for Jesse Jackson.

NEW YORK VICE

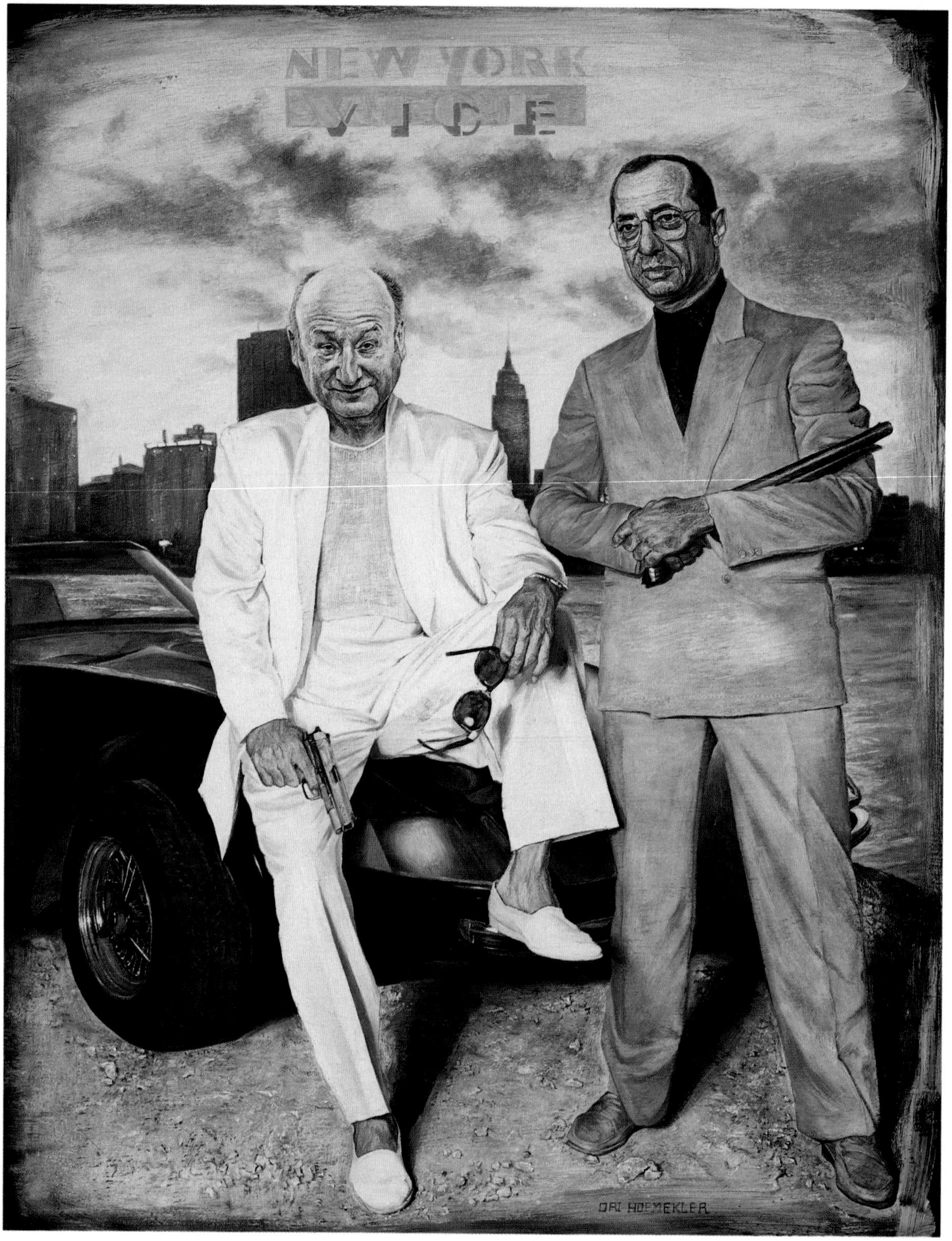
NEW YORK
VICE

ED KOCH, MAYOR OF NEW YORK CITY, AND
MARIO CUOMO, GOVERNOR OF NEW YORK

Miami Vice is America's most popular TV show. It reflects America's self-image today in its fashion—the dress, the poses, the music. Also back in fashion is the traditional hero, who stands with a gun in his hands shooting everyone. The good guys off the bad guys. The producers want to show life to be beautiful (on the surface), so they show it sterilized. The fashions, guns, sunsets, everything in the show is beautiful. Of course we're hardly dealing with reality; what is important, though, is that the show is popular.

I thought, Why the hell Miami, when most of the world is actually in New York? In my show, Koch is Crockett and Cuomo is Tubbs. Both of them are supposed to take care of New York, like the two guys from the TV show are supposed to take care of Miami.

It seemed to me that if Koch and Cuomo were a *Miami Vice* episode, Koch, a clown, would want to take Johnson's role, since he is the sexiest guy in America. Cuomo is serious—he wants to be president. And Koch's and Cuomo's pleasure with the piece, as well as its popularity, proves that anything can happen.

THE HONEYMOONERS

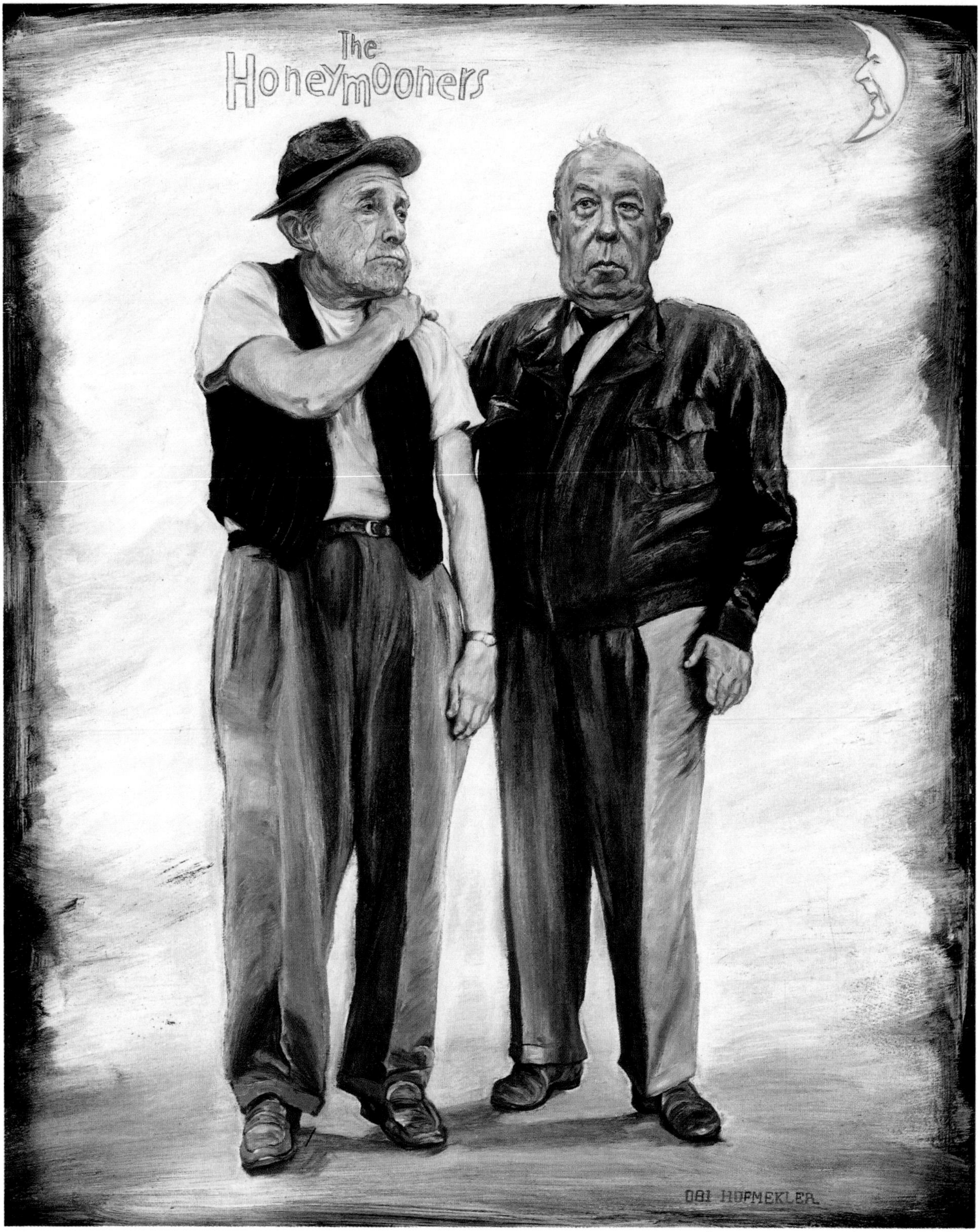
The
Honeymooners
OBI HOFMEKLER

GEORGE SHULTZ, U.S. SECRETARY OF STATE, AND
CASPAR WEINBERGER, U.S. SECRETARY OF DEFENSE

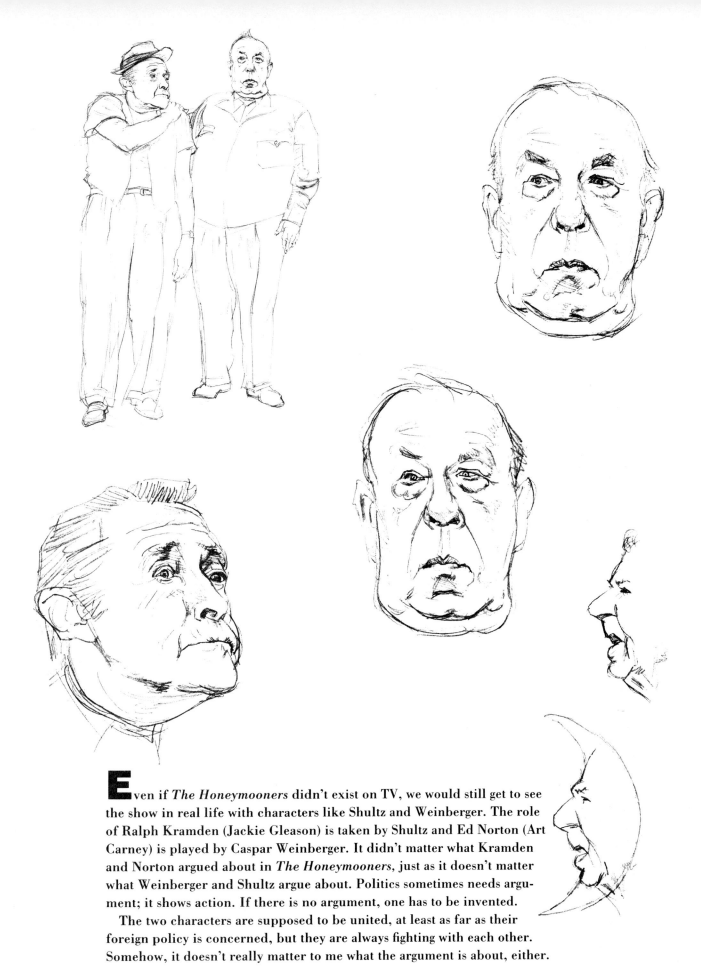

Even if *The Honeymooners* didn't exist on TV, we would still get to see
the show in real life with characters like Shultz and Weinberger. The role
of Ralph Kramden (Jackie Gleason) is taken by Shultz and Ed Norton (Art
Carney) is played by Caspar Weinberger. It didn't matter what Kramden
and Norton argued about in *The Honeymooners*, just as it doesn't matter
what Weinberger and Shultz argue about. Politics sometimes needs argument; it shows action. If there is no argument, one has to be invented.

The two characters are supposed to be united, at least as far as their
foreign policy is concerned, but they are always fighting with each other.
Somehow, it doesn't really matter to me what the argument is about, either.

THRILLERS

THE BIRDS

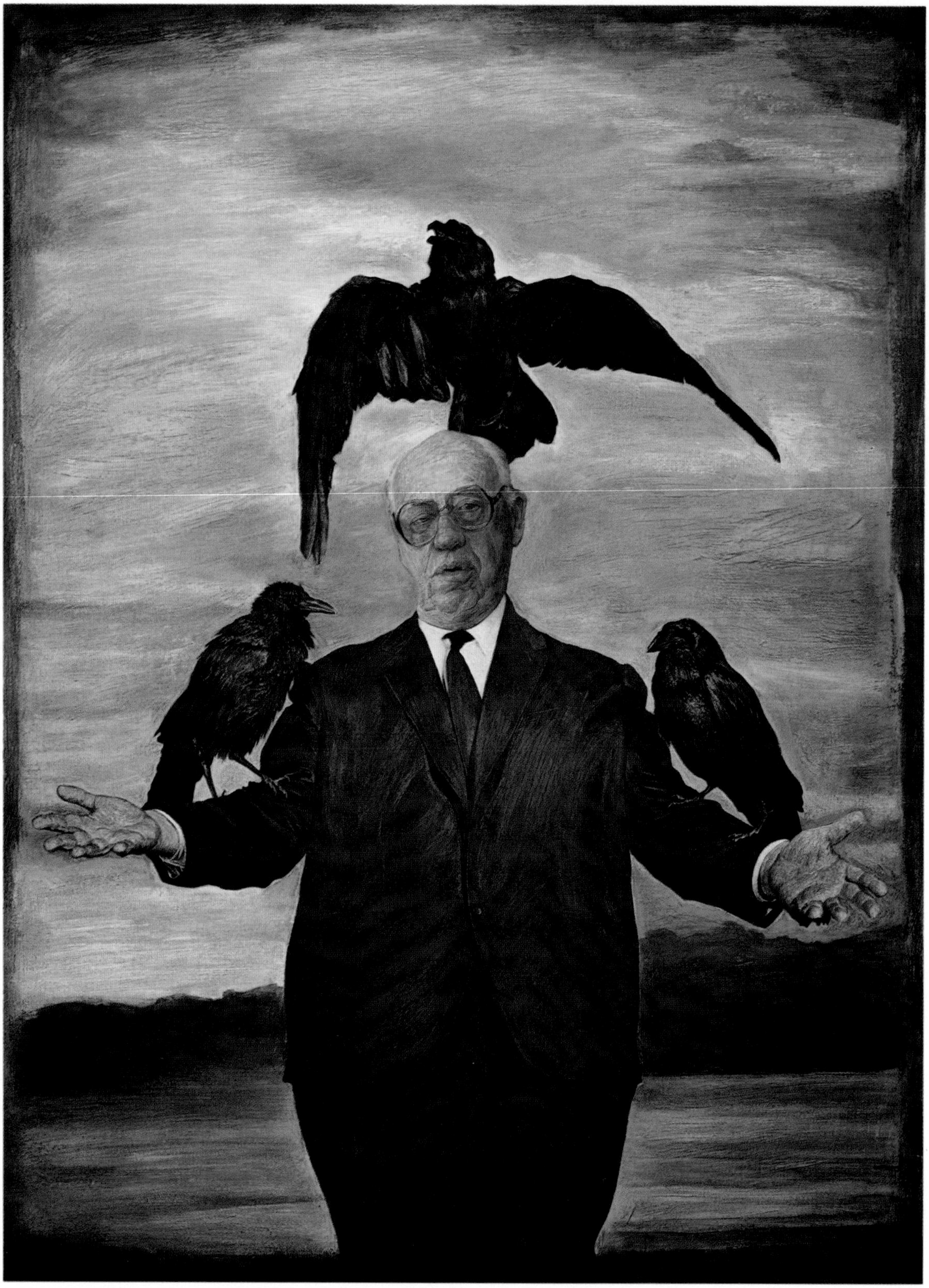

WILLIAM J. CASEY, FORMER DIRECTOR OF THE C.I.A.

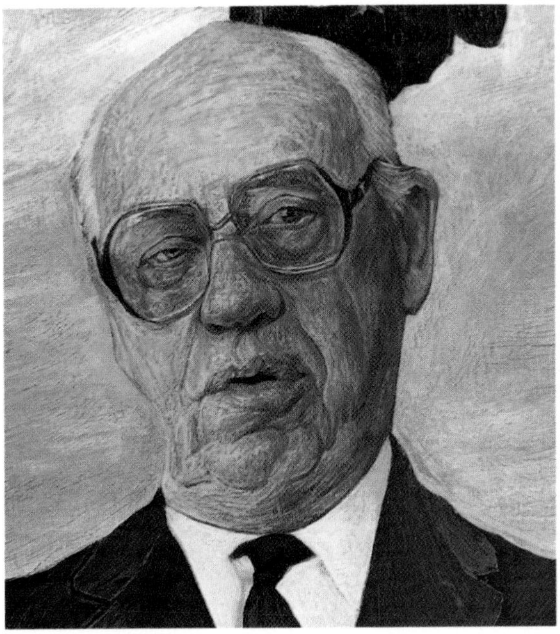

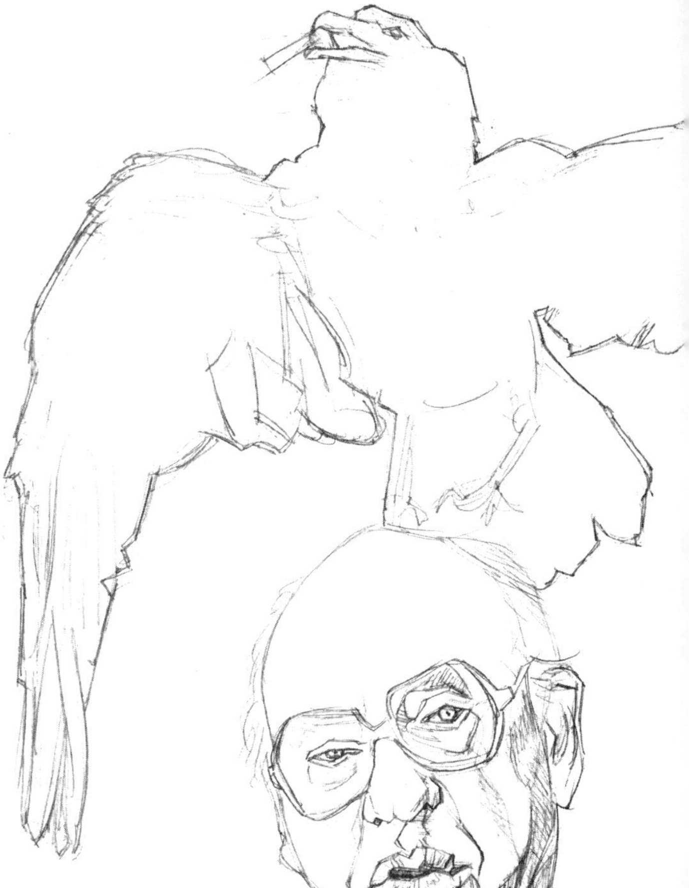

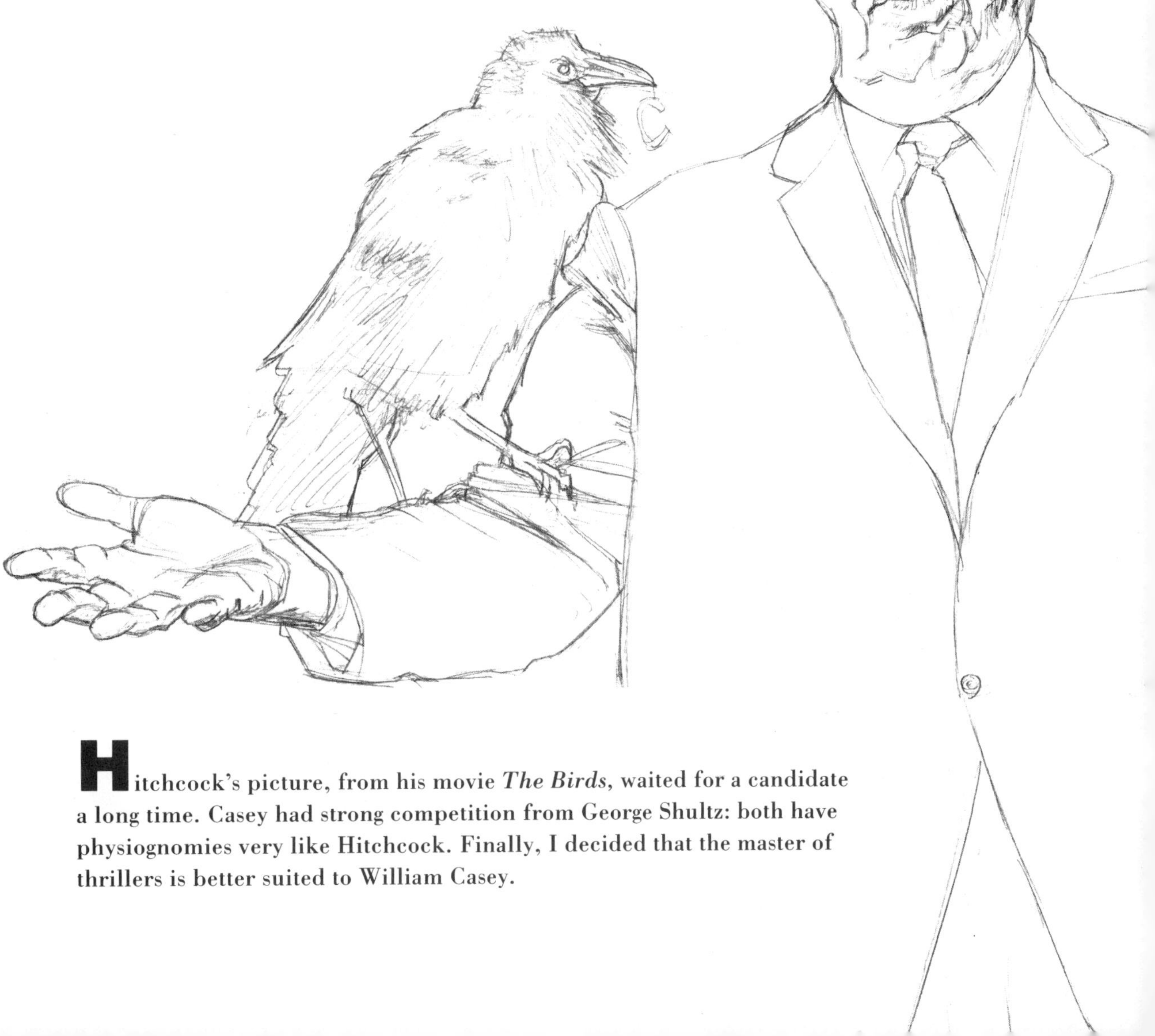

Hitchcock's picture, from his movie *The Birds*, waited for a candidate a long time. Casey had strong competition from George Shultz: both have physiognomies very like Hitchcock. Finally, I decided that the master of thrillers is better suited to William Casey.

FRANKENSTEIN

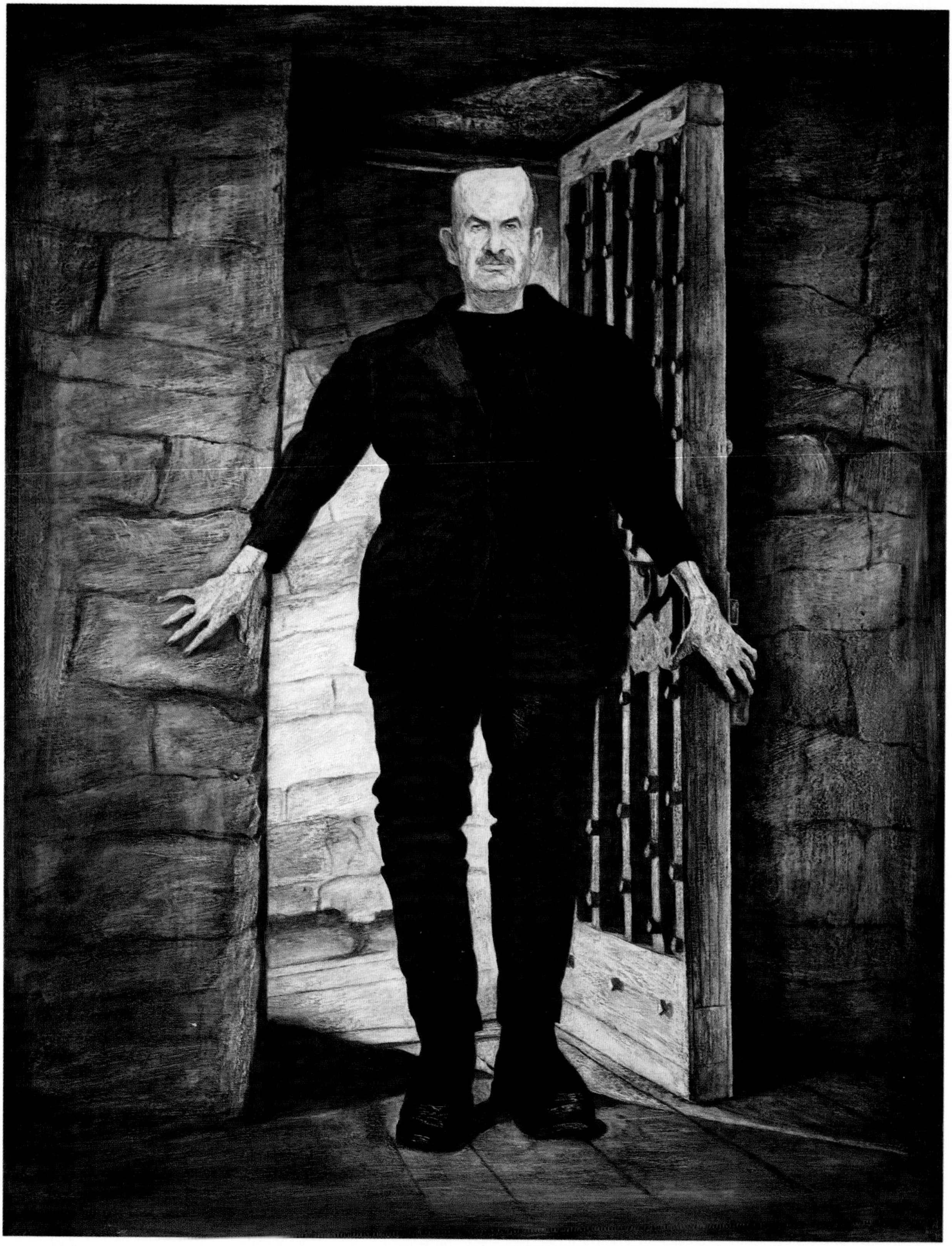

HAFIZ ASSAD, PRESIDENT OF SYRIA

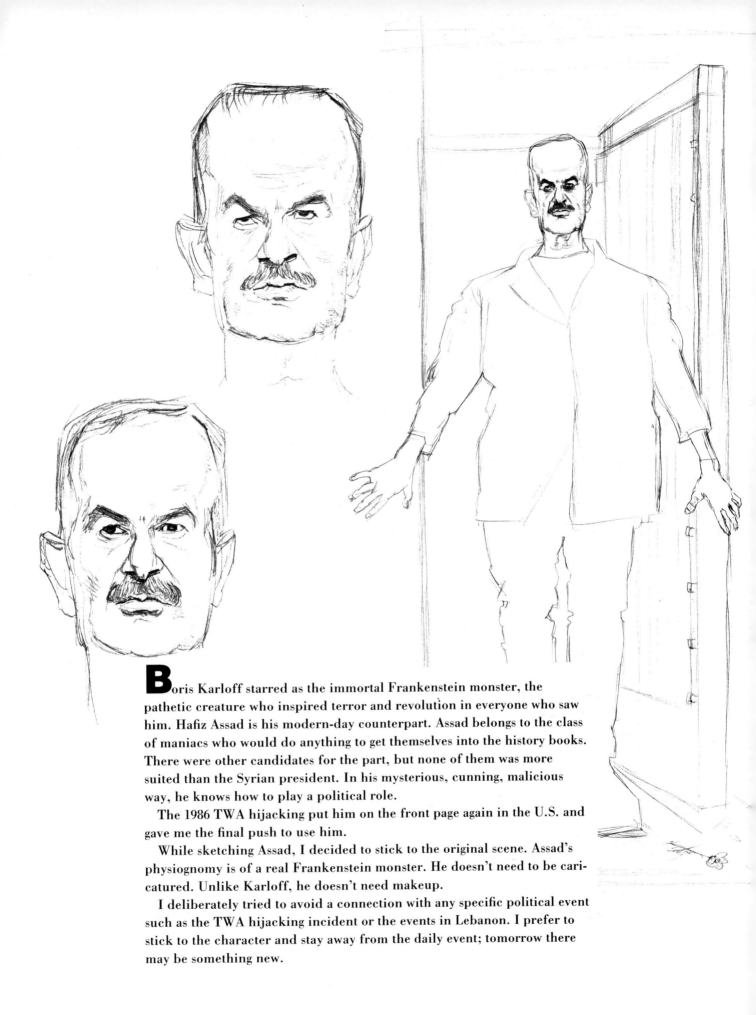

Boris Karloff starred as the immortal Frankenstein monster, the pathetic creature who inspired terror and revolution in everyone who saw him. Hafiz Assad is his modern-day counterpart. Assad belongs to the class of maniacs who would do anything to get themselves into the history books. There were other candidates for the part, but none of them was more suited than the Syrian president. In his mysterious, cunning, malicious way, he knows how to play a political role.

The 1986 TWA hijacking put him on the front page again in the U.S. and gave me the final push to use him.

While sketching Assad, I decided to stick to the original scene. Assad's physiognomy is of a real Frankenstein monster. He doesn't need to be caricatured. Unlike Karloff, he doesn't need makeup.

I deliberately tried to avoid a connection with any specific political event such as the TWA hijacking incident or the events in Lebanon. I prefer to stick to the character and stay away from the daily event; tomorrow there may be something new.

DRACULA

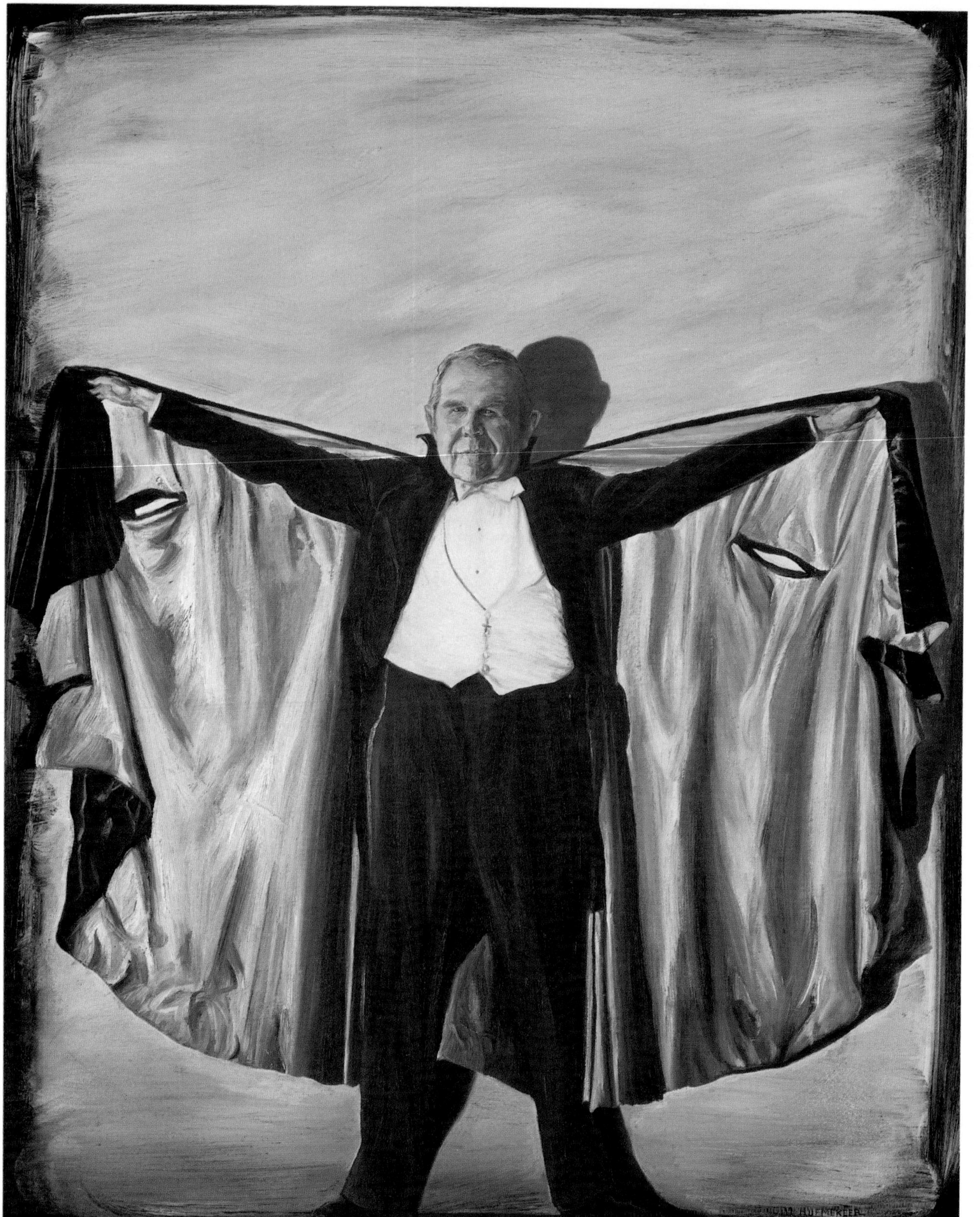

PAT ROBERTSON, TV EVANGELIST

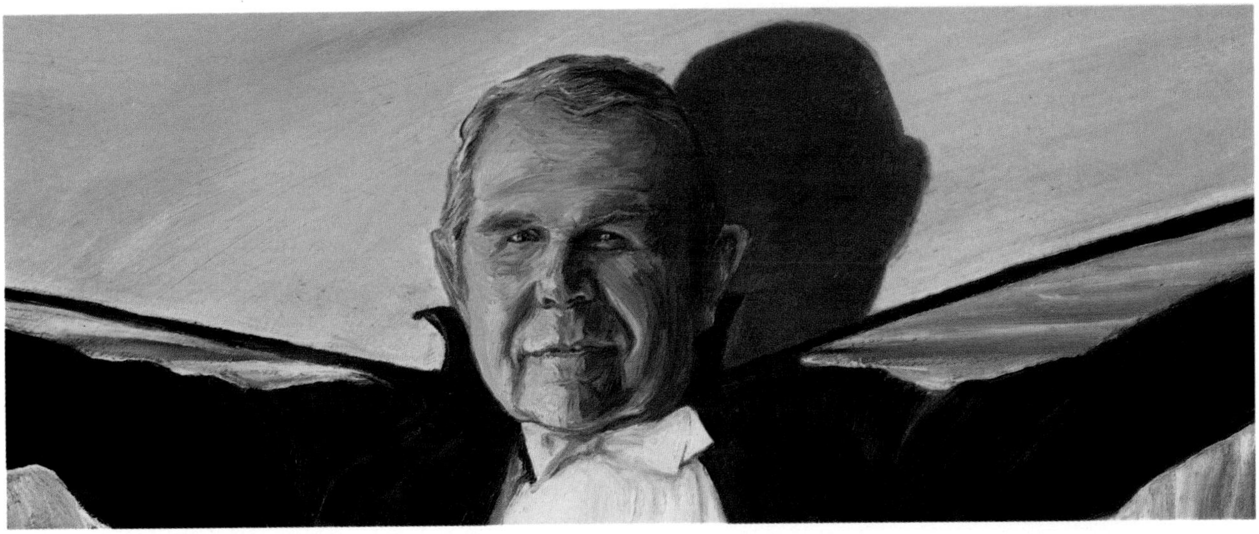

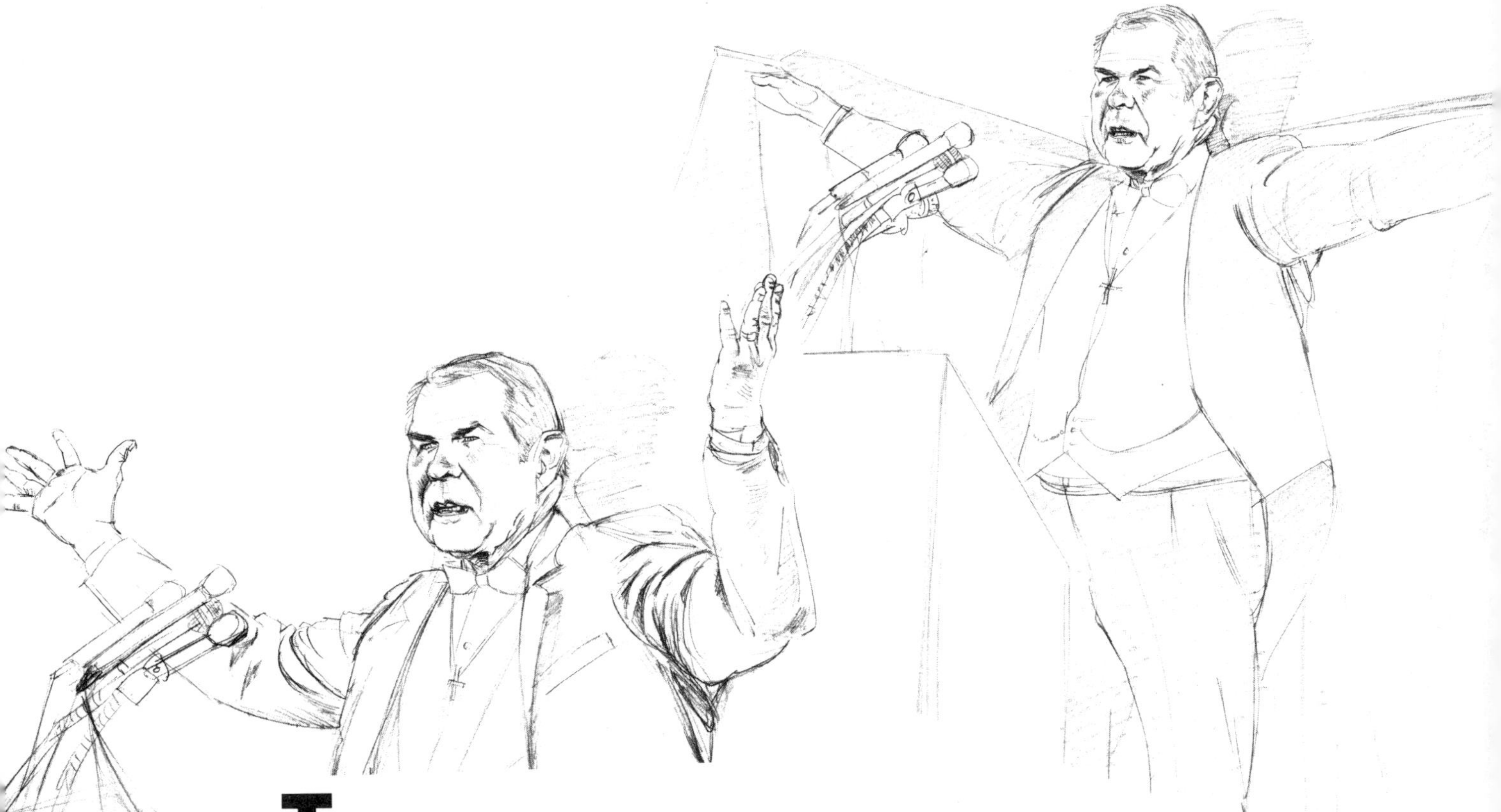

This piece was commissioned by the *New Republic* for a cover story on the increasing influence of evangelists in America.

Eschewing sex because it didn't seem right in that context, I had no choice but to do a realistic picture showing Pat Robertson as he is.

With Dracula as a model, I didn't have to change much. (Robertson often wears a black tuxedo.) To me, his performance owes a lot to witchcraft. Like Dracula, he seems to patronize his audience, and to be equally alluring. They react differently to the cross, however.

I like to satirize such men because a sense of humor doesn't seem to be their strong point.

DOCTOR MABUSE

THE ECONOMIC SUMMIT OF WESTERN LEADERS

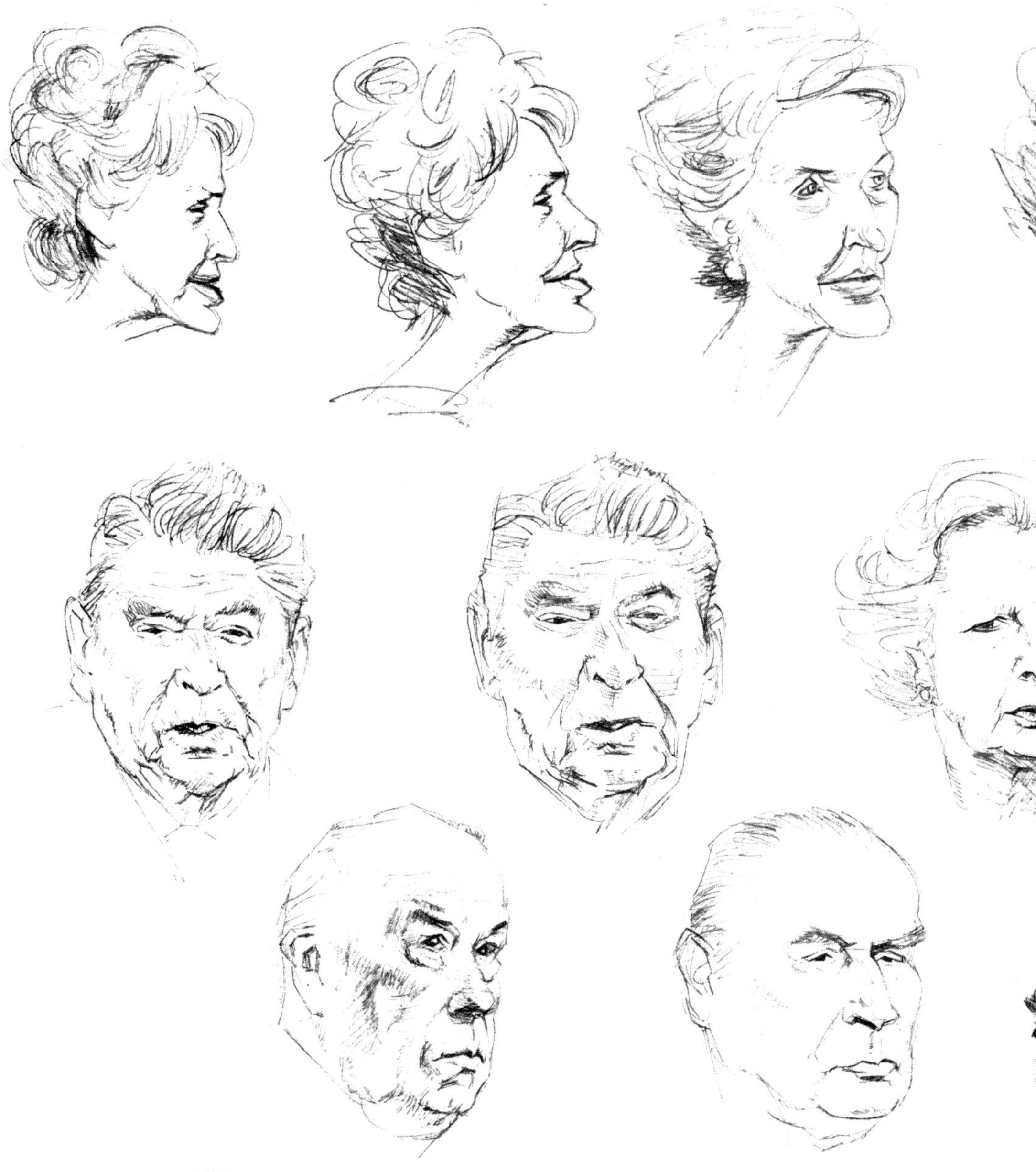

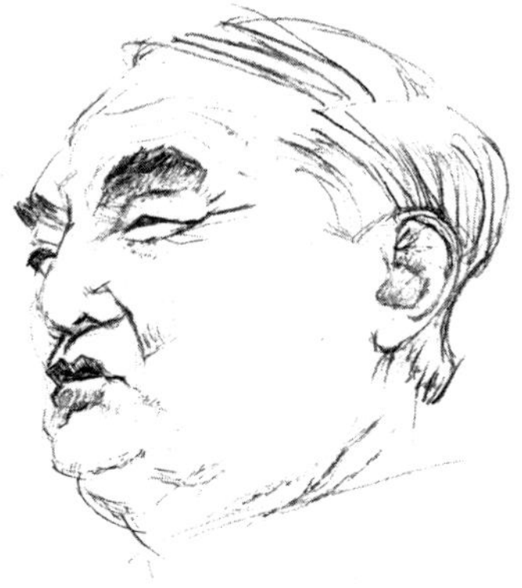

Fritz Lang directed *Doctor Mabuse* in 1922, before the economic catastrophe and the monumental crash of the New York stock market.

Doctor Mabuse is an international crook who uses his power and any other means to get money. The movie parallels what looks to me almost like a rule of thumb for certain politicians: Politics requires money in order to gain power in order to make money in order to have more power in order to make more money in order to buy more power . . .

The opening scene from the movie is a séance. I chose this scene for the summit meeting of the leaders of the Western World. As in the movie, in reality there is a mythical, mystic admiration for money and a pathetic adoration of power.

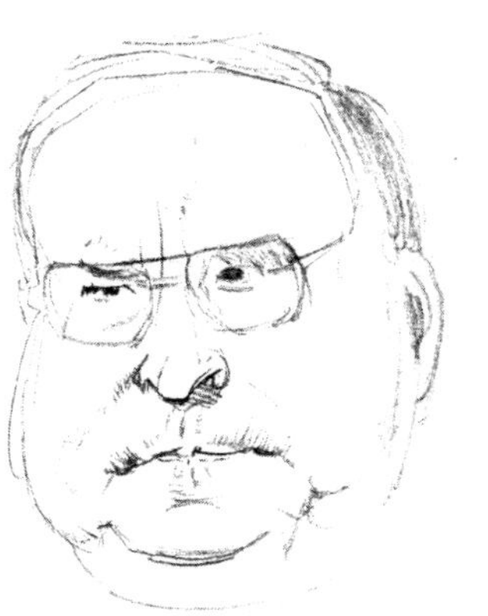

In my drawing, in the middle of the table there is a dollar bill—one buck. As banal as it sounds, when I think about it, I truly believe that the dollar bill is taking on a more and more mystical dimension. That's why the summit leaders are trying to appeal to the money ghost.

ROSEMARY'S BABY

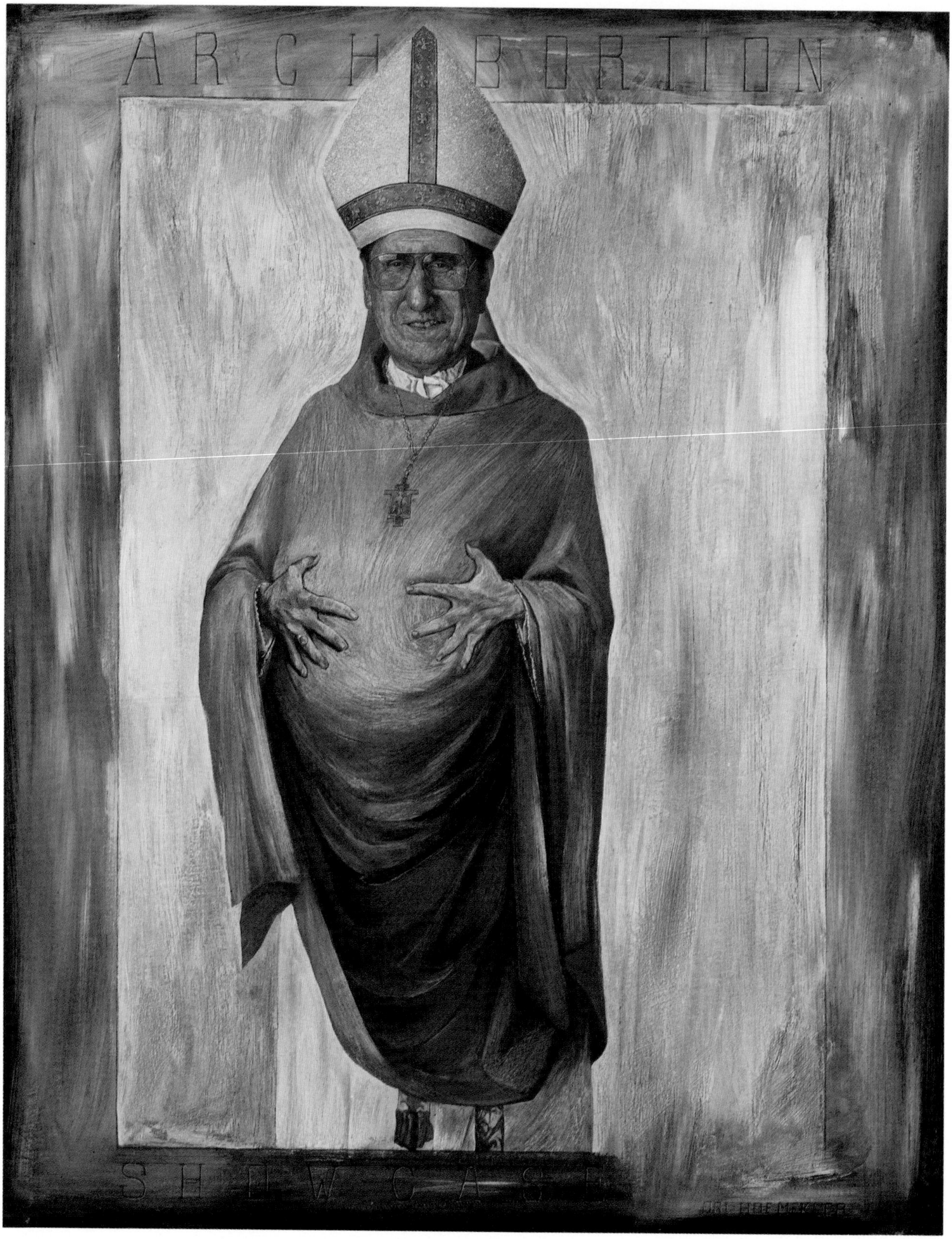
ARCH BORTION
SHOWCASE

ARCHBISHOP JOHN J. O'CONNOR

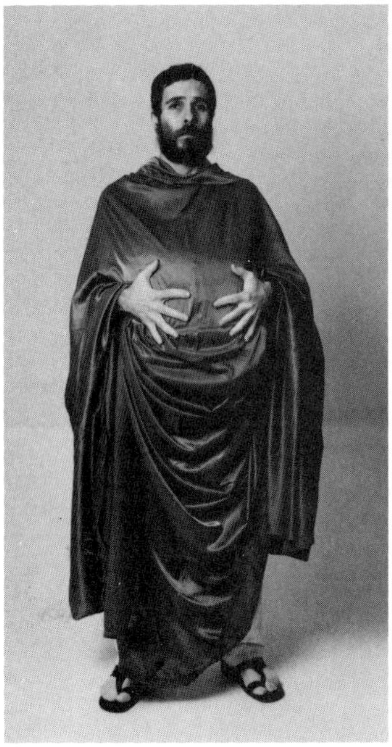

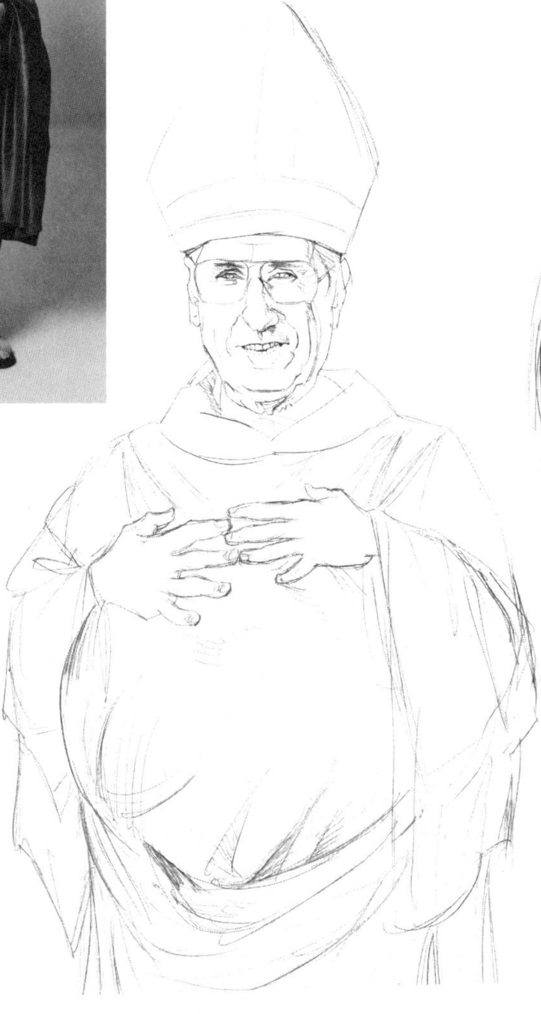

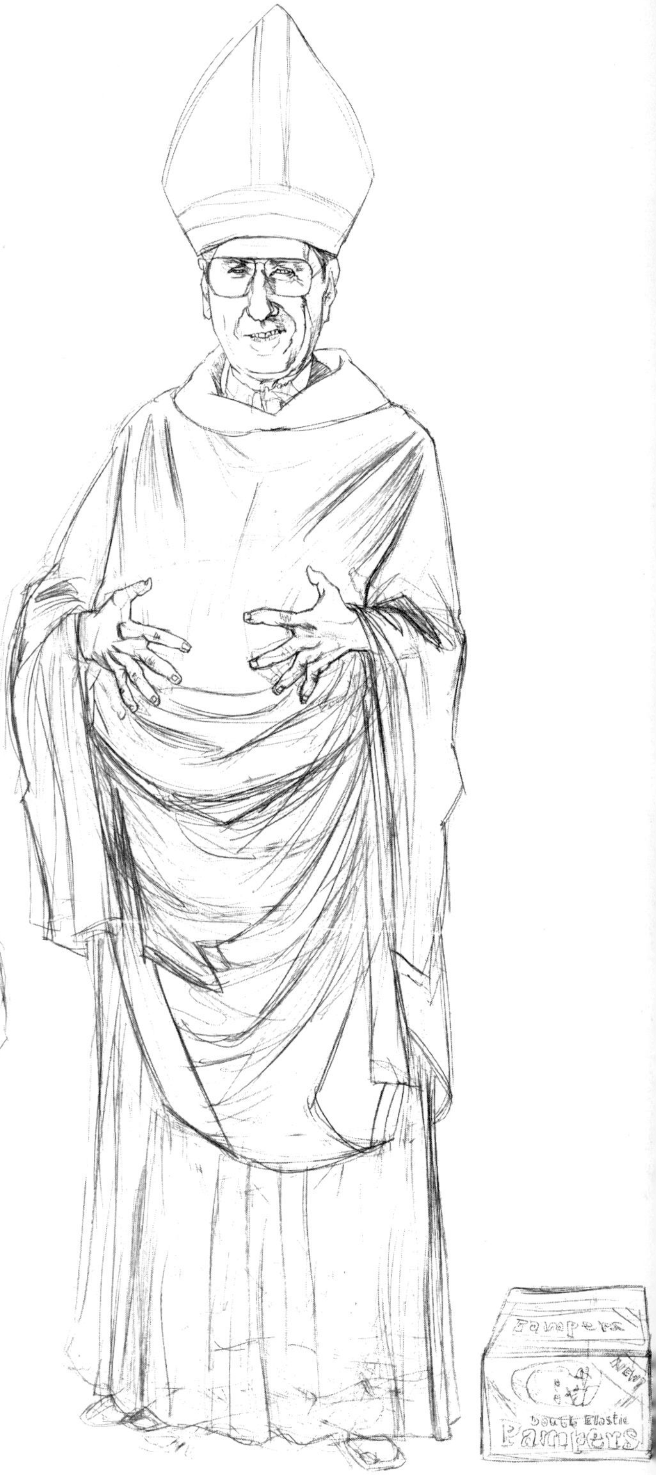
Pampers

***R**osemary's Baby*, a combination of pregnancy, religion, and politics, was a thriller.

When Archbishop O'Connor rails against abortion, he means to take away the right of a woman to maintain control over her own body.

In my show, the archbishop is pregnant. Since this is an immaculate conception, the question of who the father is is moot. The main point is that O'Connor is going to have a baby and if there's a law against abortion there's nothing to be done about it.

I think that in a way the archbishop *is* actually pregnant. His baby is the antiabortion movement.

CLASSIC
ART

BOTTICELLI'S "BIRTH OF VENUS"

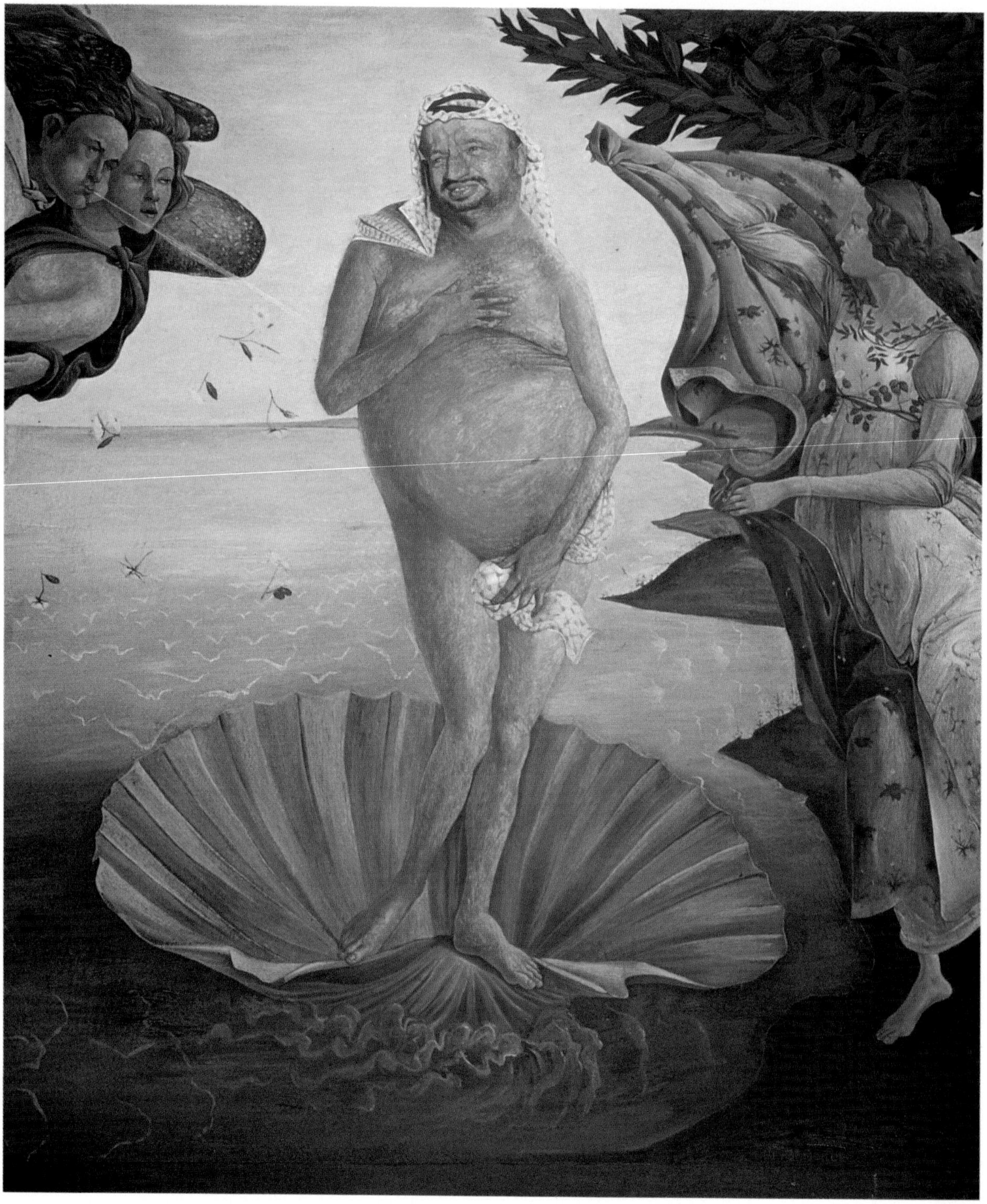

YASIR ARAFAT, CHAIRMAN OF THE P.L.O.

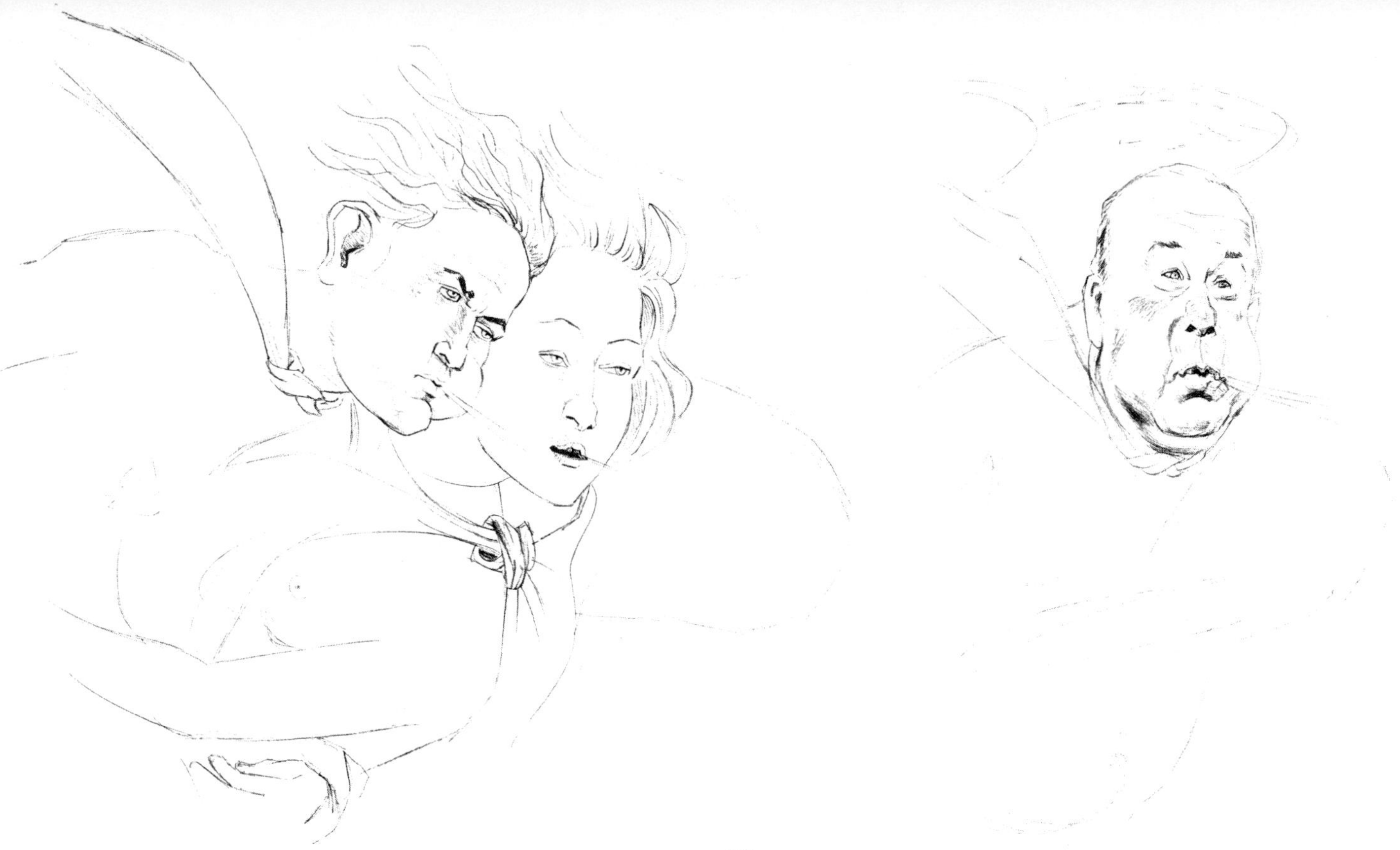

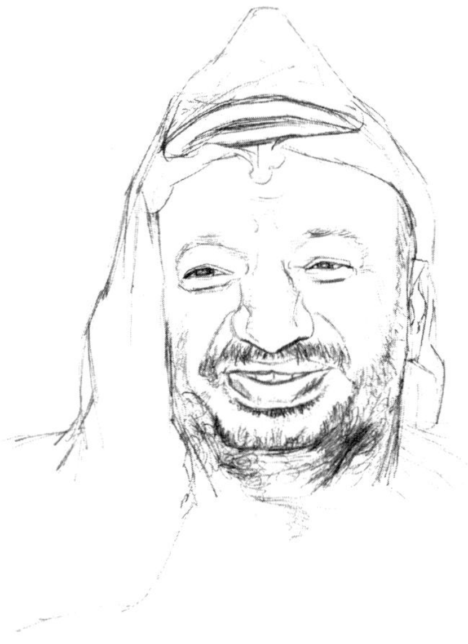

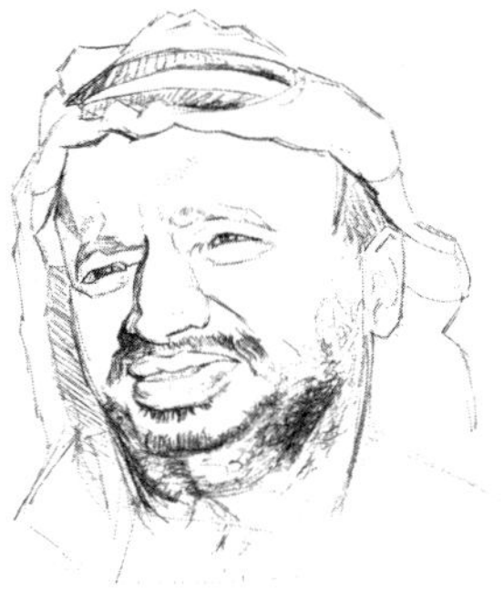

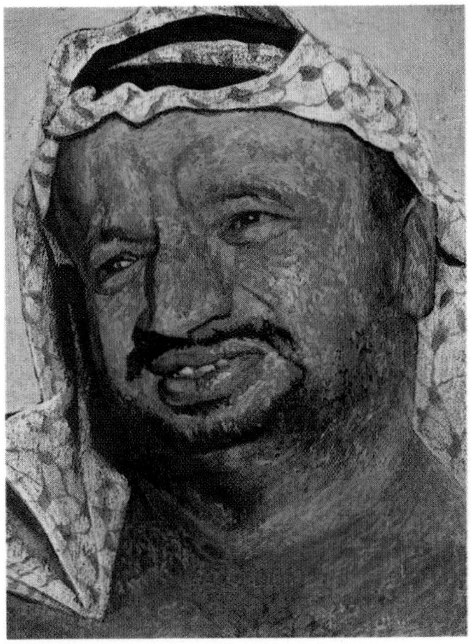

Arafat was haunted by the Syrians and by his own people during the Lebanon War. The Palestinian leader's image had been changed to that of an underdog. He started to talk differently. He was almost a peacemaker.

I've put Arafat in a Botticelli picture to give him a new chance. I tried to stay close to the original Venus. Venus's birth is a symbol of renewal. Botticelli's works are on the edge of kitsch. They are clean, illustrated ideals, almost caricatures.

I just gave Arafat a chance for once to play the role of the most beautiful lady. My apologies to Botticelli.

MICHELANGELO'S SISTINE CHAPEL
—"THE CREATION OF ADAM"

REVEREND JERRY FALWELL,
LEADER OF THE MORAL MAJORITY

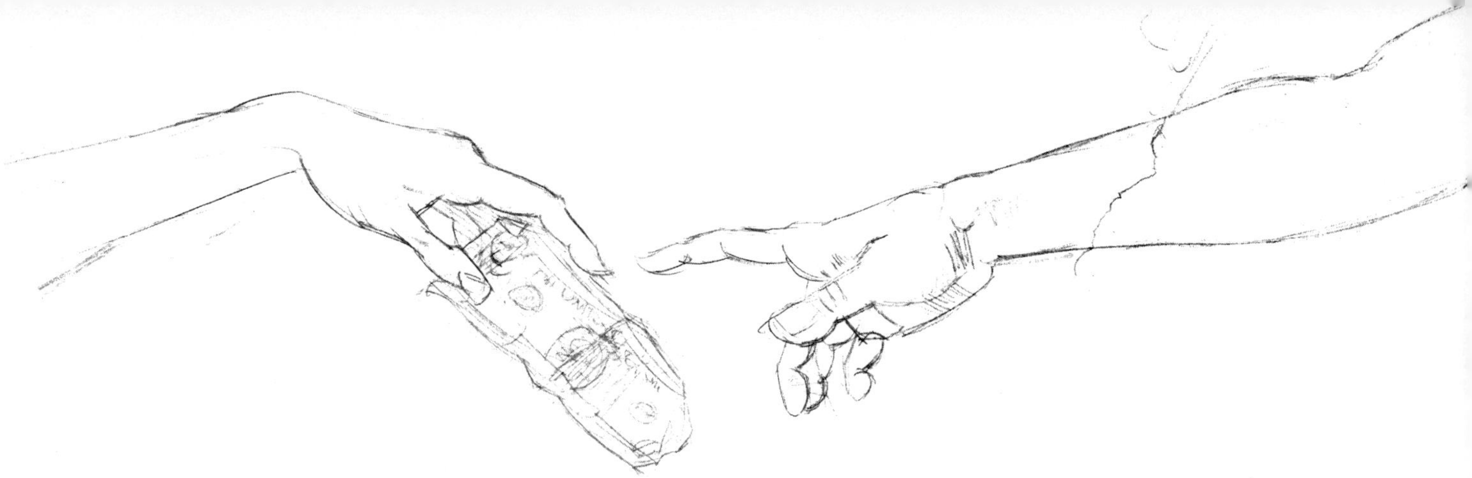

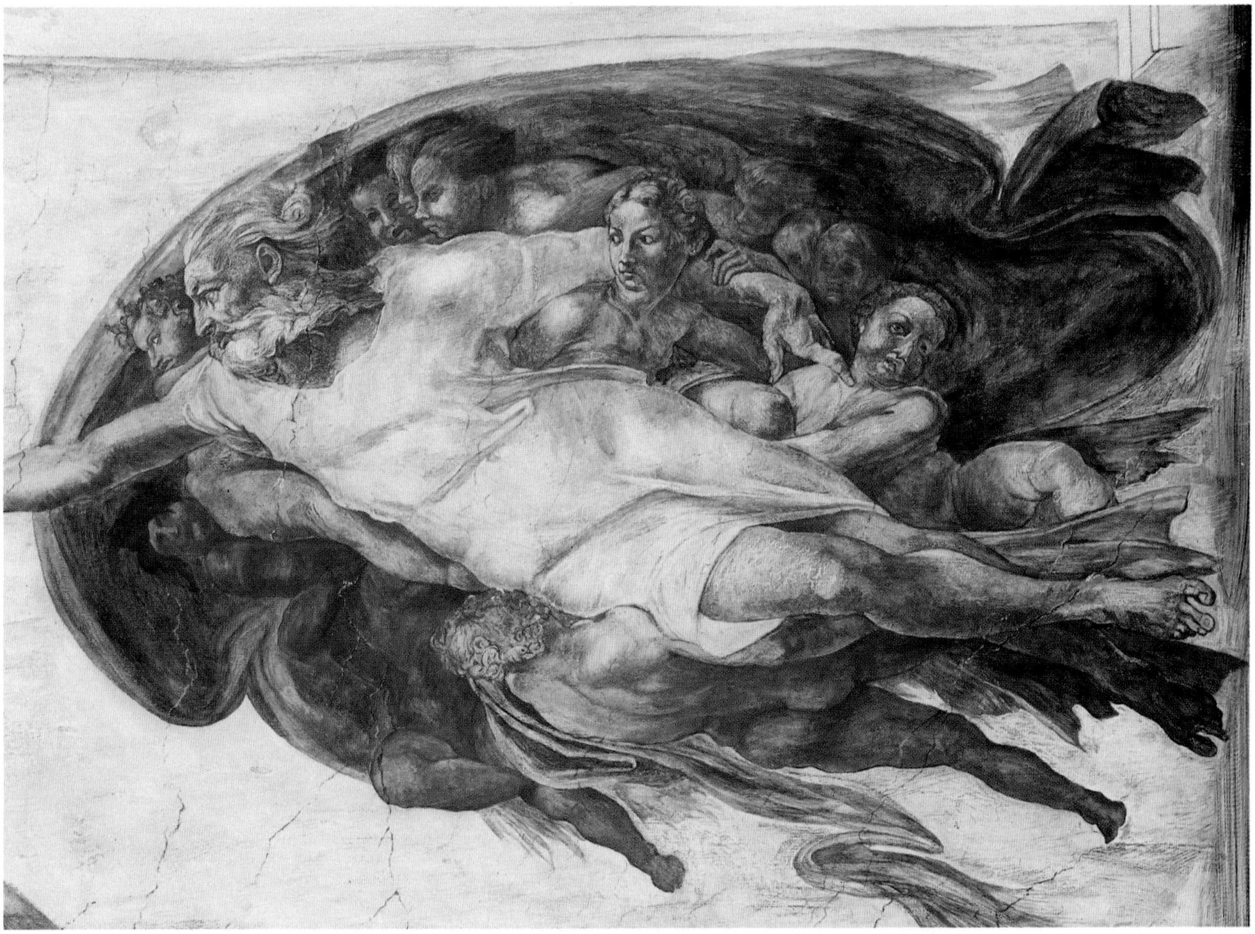

Moral Majority leader Jerry Falwell is the most famous TV evangelist. Falwell and his friends are making money through TV by licensing the Holy Spirit to anyone who is ready to pay. The combination of money, religion and politics is always dangerous.

In order to make his case, Reverend Falwell needs powerful imagery. Here he is taking the role of Adam in the Sistine Chapel fresco *The Creation of Adam.* I deliberately tried to be as faithful to the original as possible. The only change is that Reverend Falwell doesn't have the athletic body of Michelangelo's Adam. The dollar bill between Falwell and God is the only addition to the original.

RODIN'S "THE THINKER"

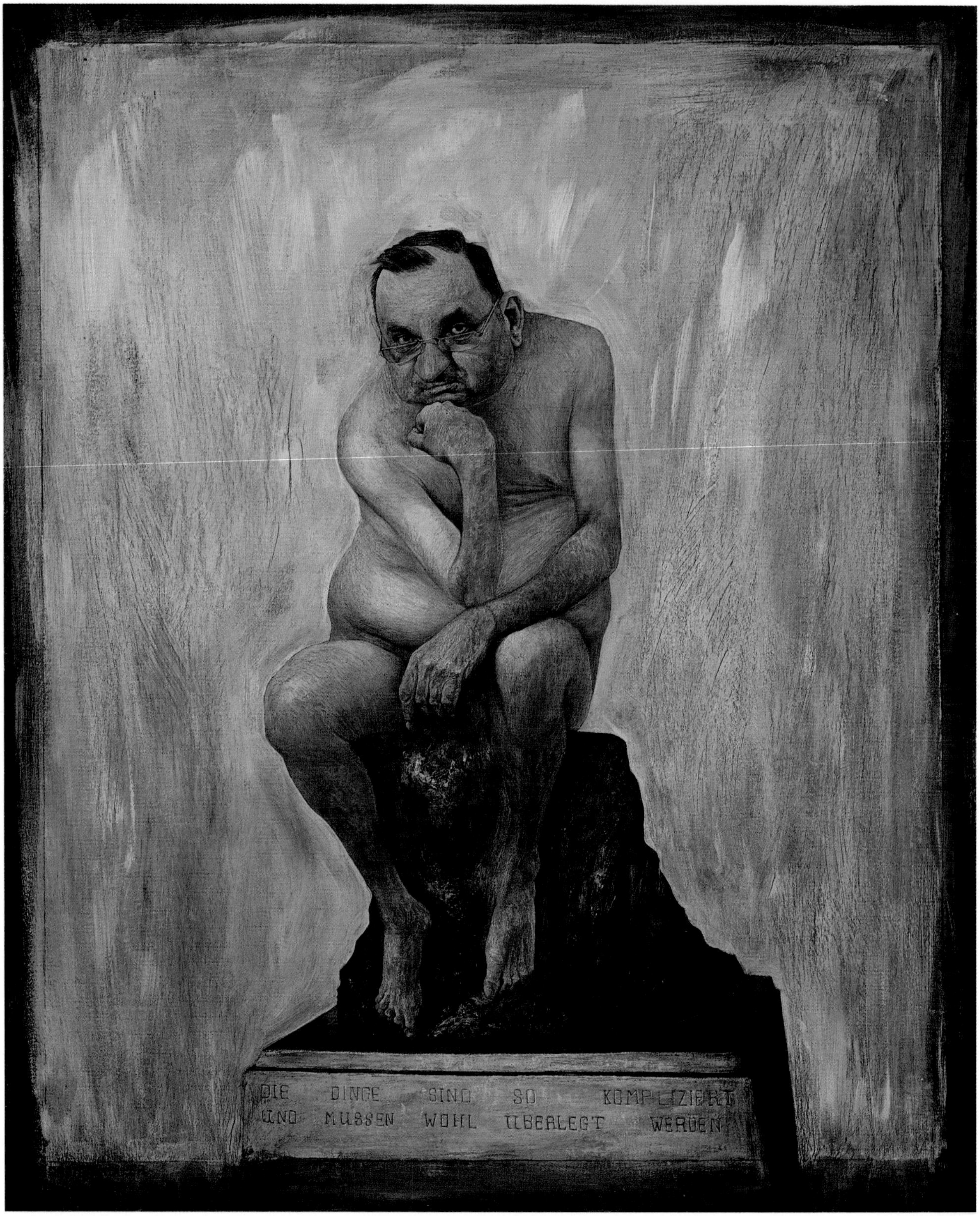
DIE DINGE SIND SO KOMPLIZIERT
UND MUSSEN WOHL UBERLEGT WERDEN

FRED SINOWATZ,
FORMER CHANCELLOR OF WEST GERMANY

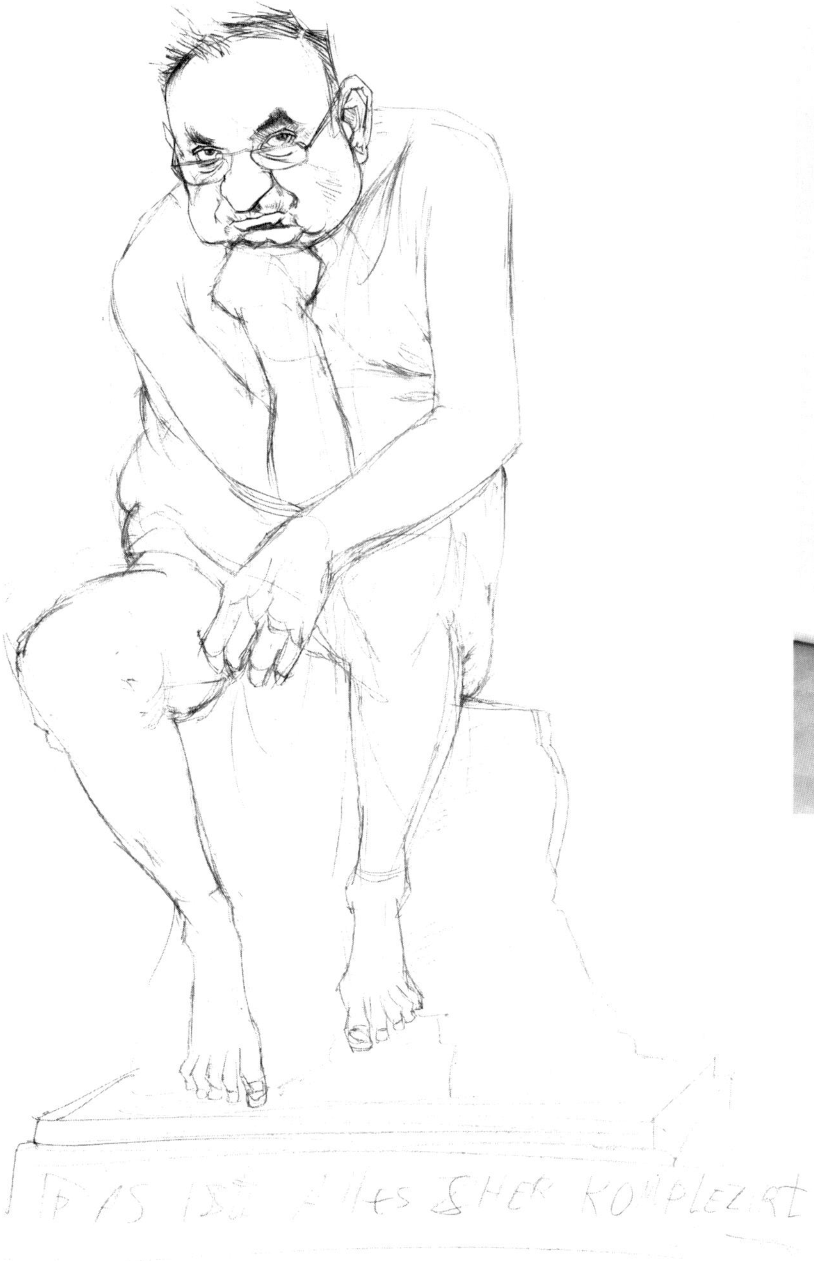
DAS IST ALLES SHER KOMPLEZIRT

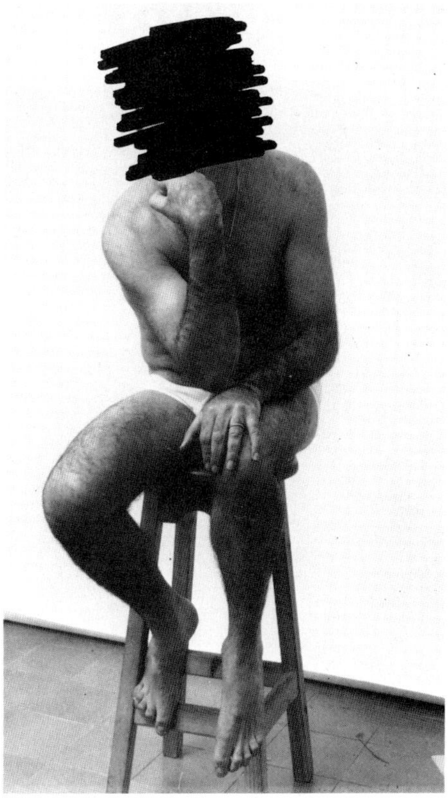

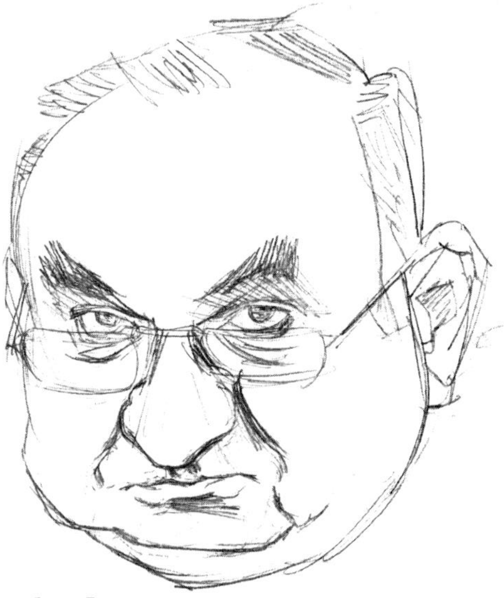

In my opinion, his was the ugliest face that ever graced my studio. I was very much stimulated to work just on his visage, which is a treasure trove of distortion.

First I was thinking of the Hunchback of Notre Dame, or a village fool by Brueghel, but I could not ignore Mr. Sinowatz's famous remark, which is always quoted in the German press: "Things are very complicated, and should be thought over." I found the comment especially pertinent after the coalition in Austria almost collapsed because of the scandal involving the defense minister. So finally I chose Rodin's *The Thinker* as the subject. My main problem was to change that handsome male figure into the flabby, paunchy, full-of-beer-and-strudel body of the former chancellor.

MICHELANGELO'S "DAVID"

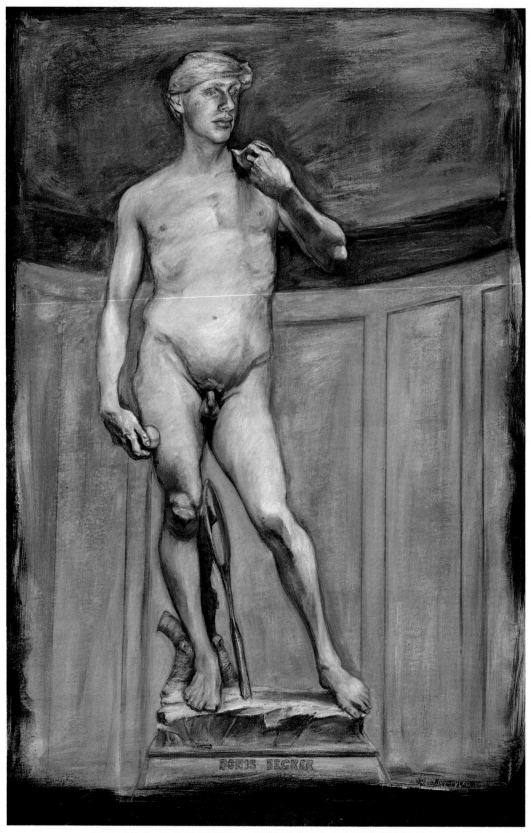

BORIS BECKER, TENNIS CHAMPION

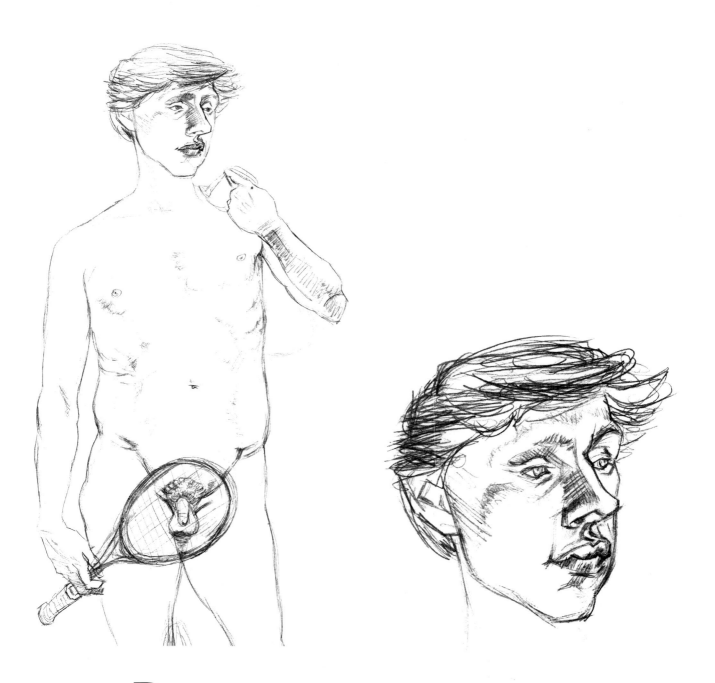

Boris Becker, a worldwide tennis champion in his teens, is already a sex symbol. In a poll in Germany, nearly half the women said they would like to have sex with him. Michelangelo's *David* shows that this is not the first time in history that a young red-haired champion was a sex symbol.

In order to put Becker in David's image, I had to make some changes on his body. Becker is not as muscular as the original *David*, but on the whole, I tried to keep as close as possible to the pose in the sculpture. It wasn't really hard, since David's hand was just waiting for five hundred years to hold a tennis racket.

Getting Becker's face without using color wasn't easy. I went through caricature on the sketches in order to understand its basic structure; I used a more open, expressive technique to avoid unnecessary details, especially on the body.

BOTTICELLI'S
"PALLAS SUBDUING A CENTAUR"

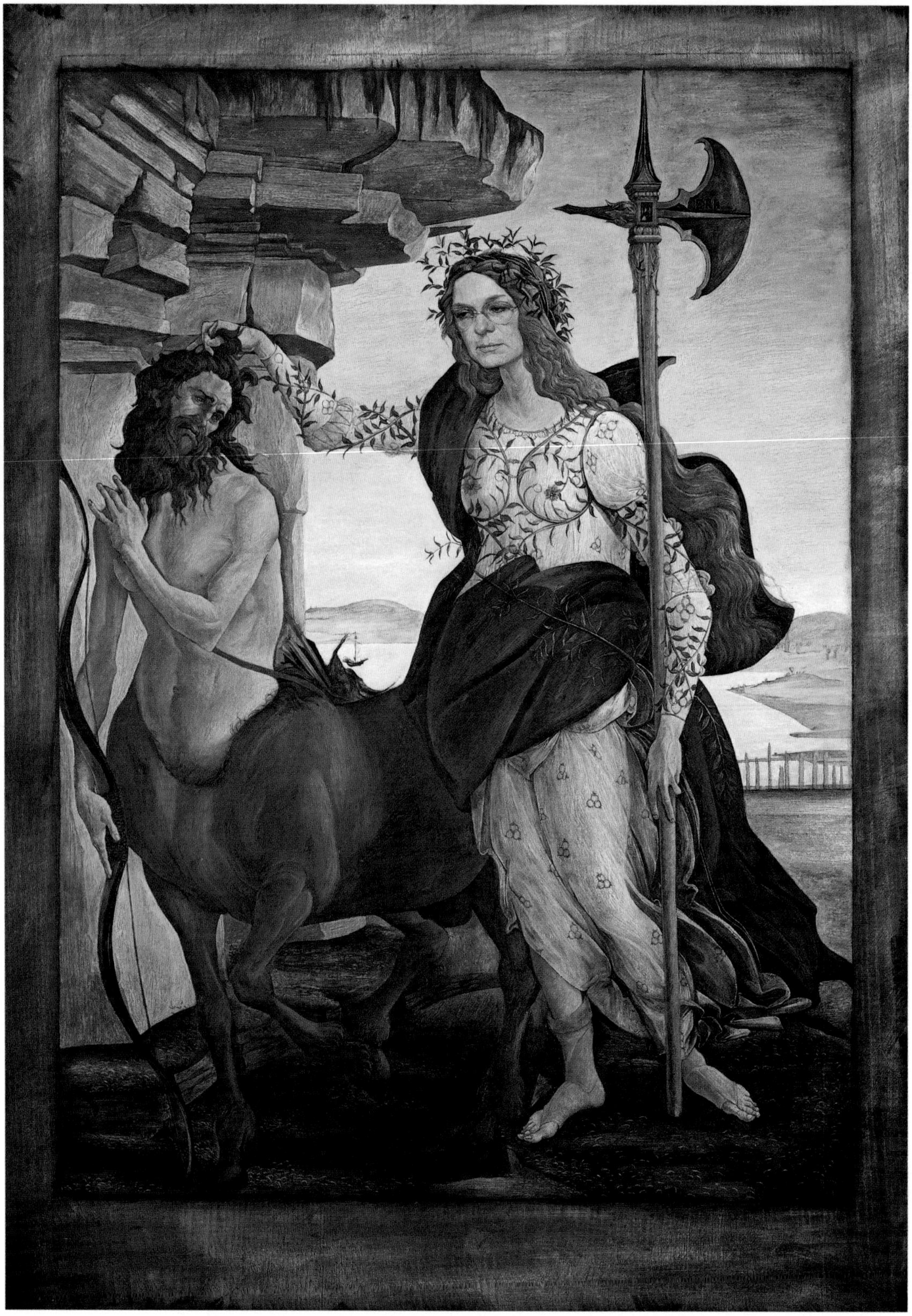

GLORIA STEINEM, FEMINIST

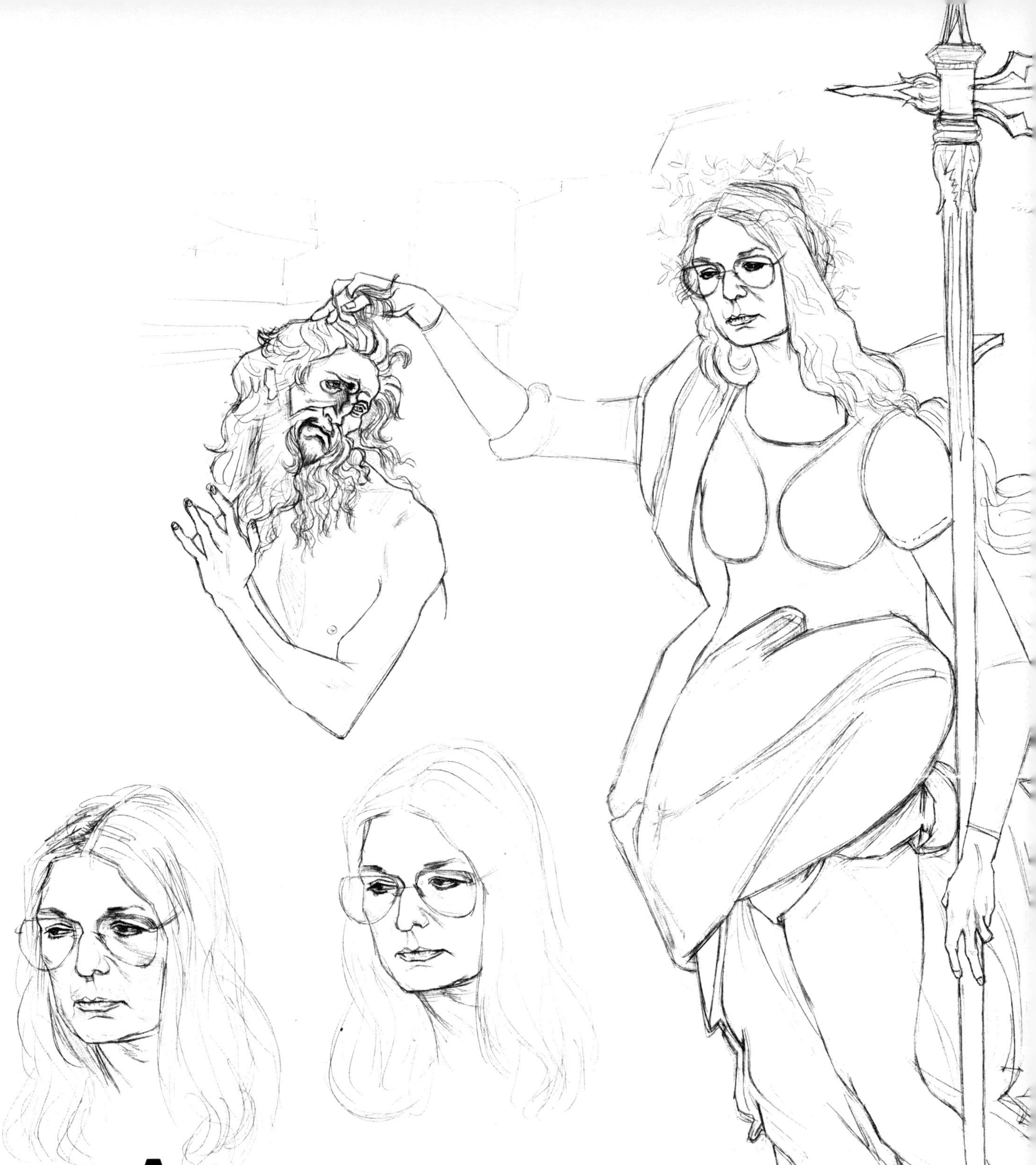

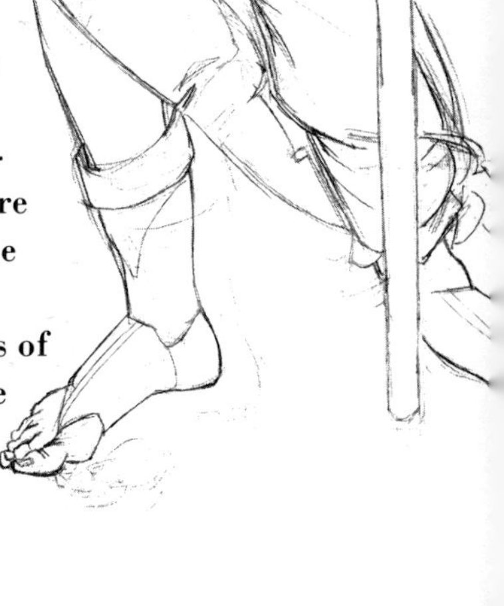

A feminist leader who is both pretty and a fighter. All characteristics that lend themselves to a stereotype.

At first I wanted to get her together with Archie Bunker. Finally I preferred to use a classic subject. It became clear to me that the feminists are not just a passing fad, but an old historic human issue. Botticelli suits me because he is one of the greatest feminists in the history of art.

Between the figure of Jael (Jael and Sisera) and Pallas Athene, goddess of war, I chose the latter, because of the direct confrontation with the male figure of the centaur.

EL GRECO'S "CRUCIFIXION"

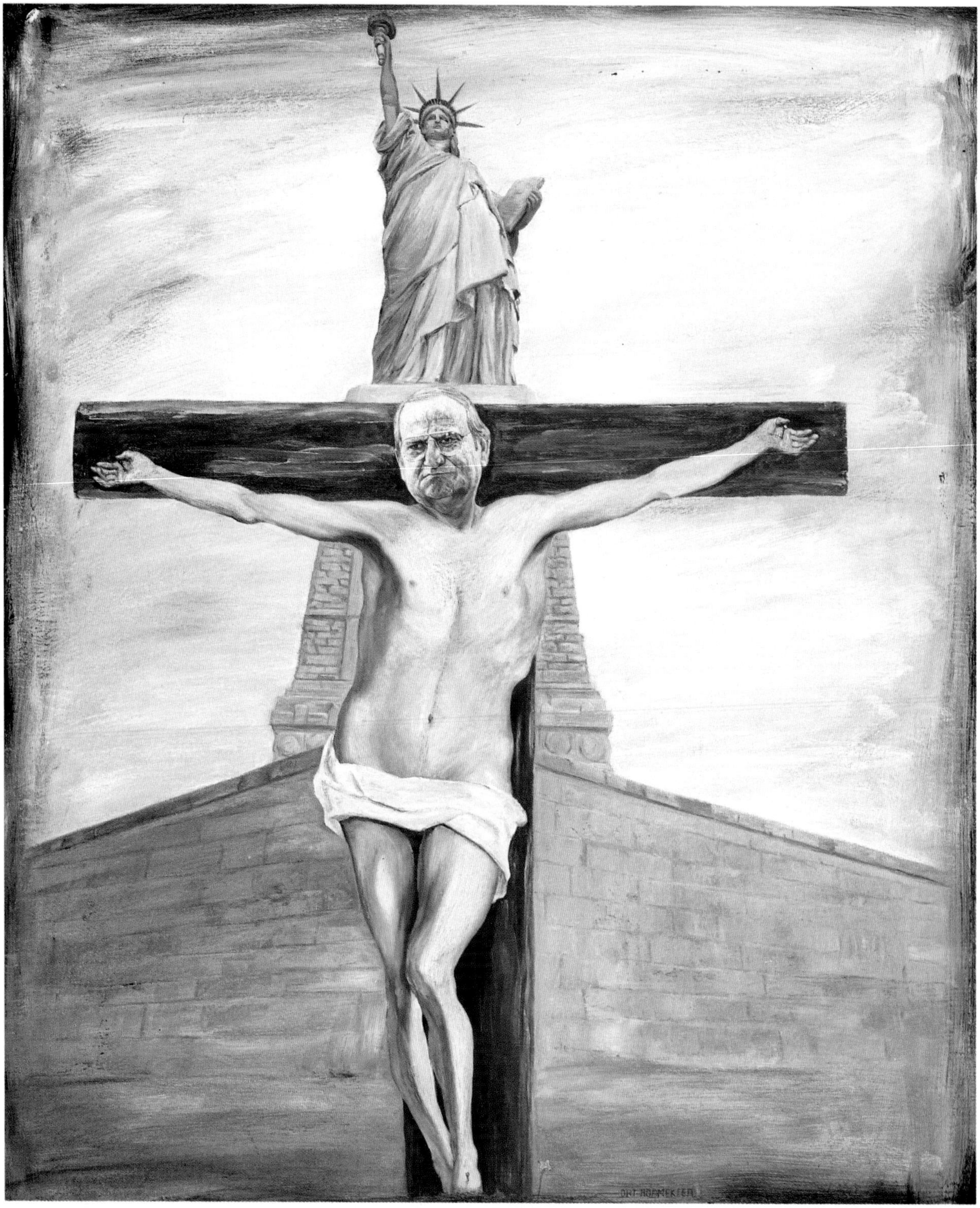

LEE IACOCCA,
CHAIRMAN OF THE CHRYSLER CORPORATION

This is the second time I've dealt with Iacocca.

Originally, I had different plans for him. While his book was a best seller, when he was so popular and people talked seriously of him as a presidential candidate, I wanted to put him in the famous classical statue of the Apollo Belvedere. The fig leaf was made into the Chrysler star logo.

My plans changed when Iacocca was fired from the Liberty Foundation. In a way, his political career was blocked, or at least he was suddenly less popular.

I was asked to do something on the Statue of Liberty celebration for a special issue of *Penthouse* magazine. When everybody was celebrating that big emotional moment, I felt that the only thing I could show was a political crucifixion on the Statue of Liberty.

BRUEGHEL'S "TRIUMPH OF DEATH"

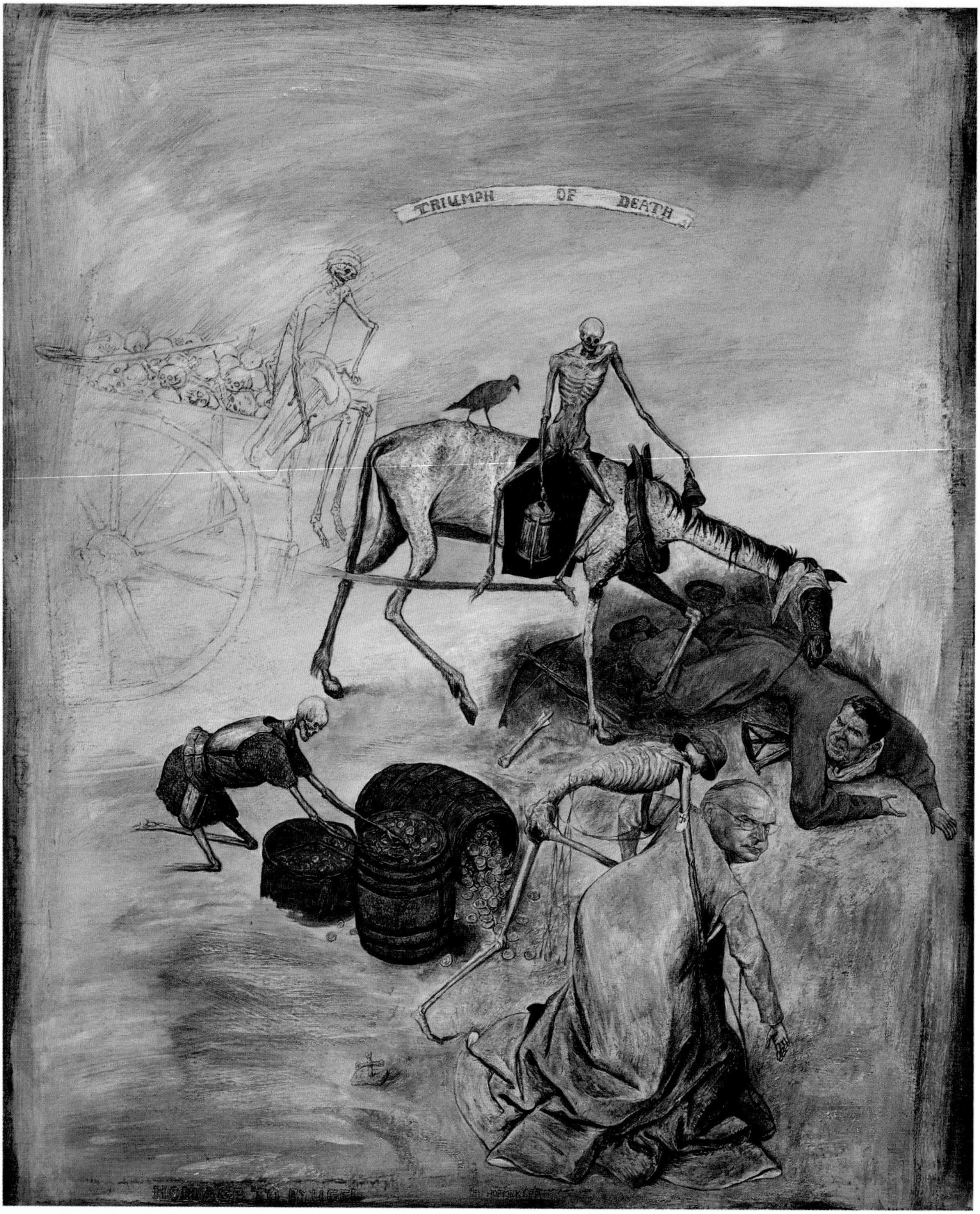
TRIUMPH OF DEATH

HELMUT KOHL, CHANCELLOR OF WEST GERMANY, AND
RONALD REAGAN, PRESIDENT OF THE UNITED STATES

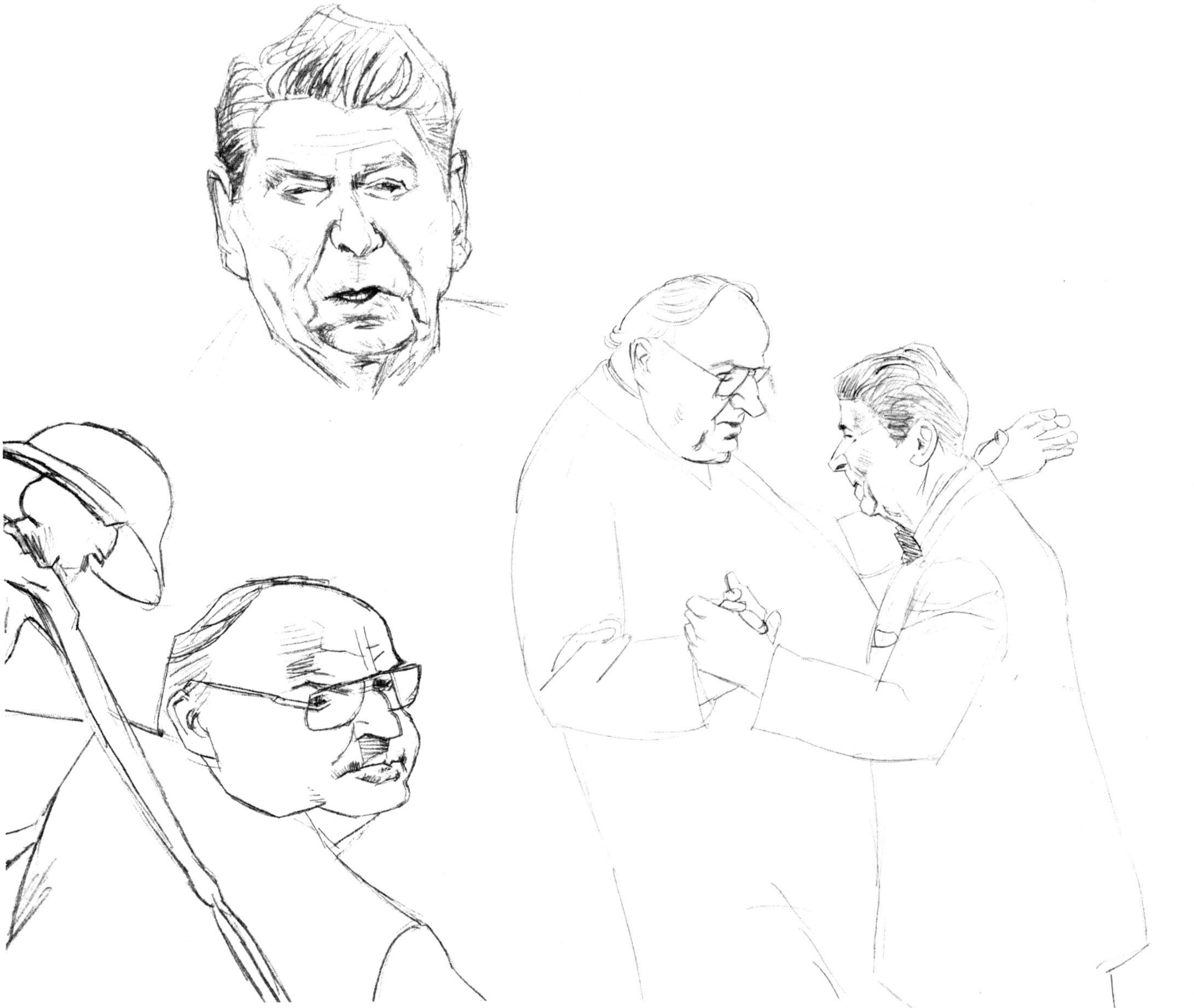

This piece was done after Reagan's visit to the Nazi cemetery in Bitburg, West Germany. My triumph of death is a confrontation between two kinds of death—one that has happened and one that is about to happen. The past is the Holocaust, and the future is nuclear catastrophe.

Death is a macabre subject, which is never easy. When I went back to Brueghel I saw that though the situation of death changes, death as a subject never does.

Brueghel pushes me to change my technique, though I feel almost intimate with his style, rhythm, and philosophy. For me, trying to imitate him, trying to break his code is like discovering a huge, intricate, mysterious secret. His composition is intuitive. I tried not to lose myself, my style, while getting inside his work.

Brueghel's painting is a damn serious one, about eternity. I wanted to take Kohl and Reagan and give them the roles in this confrontation. If Reagan is so insensitive, so ready to give up the past, god knows where he'll lead us in the nuclear future.

COMEDIES

LAUREL AND HARDY

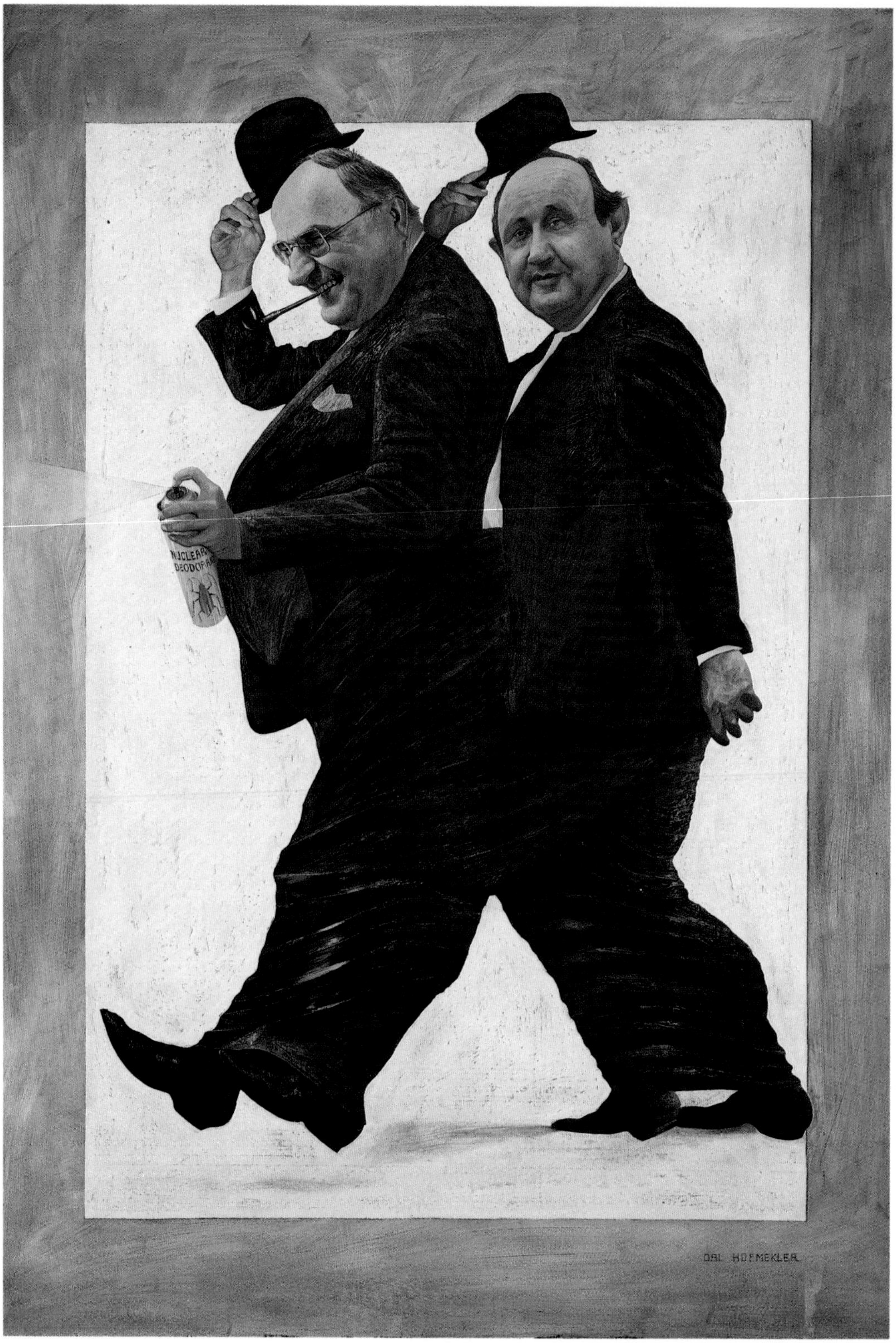

HANS-DIETRICH GENSCHER, MINISTER FOR FOREIGN AFFAIRS, AND HELMUT KOHL, CHANCELLOR OF WEST GERMANY

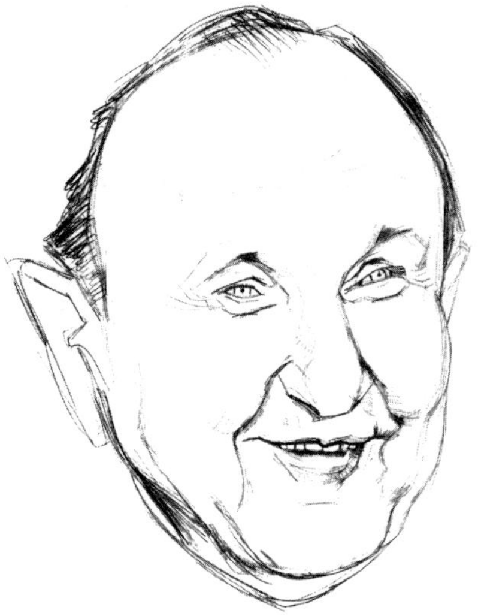

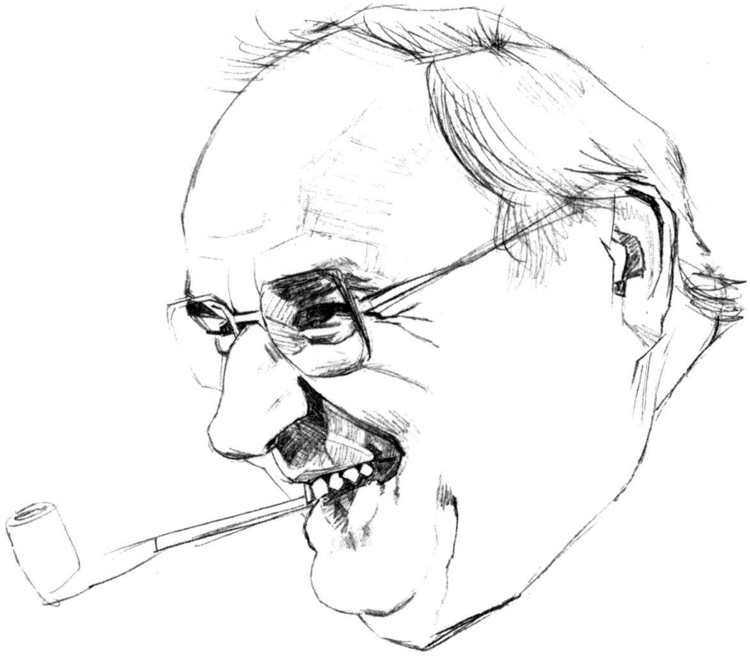

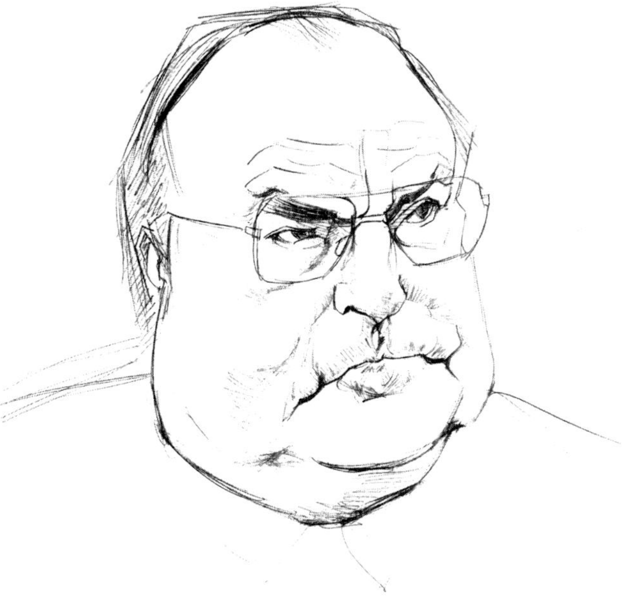

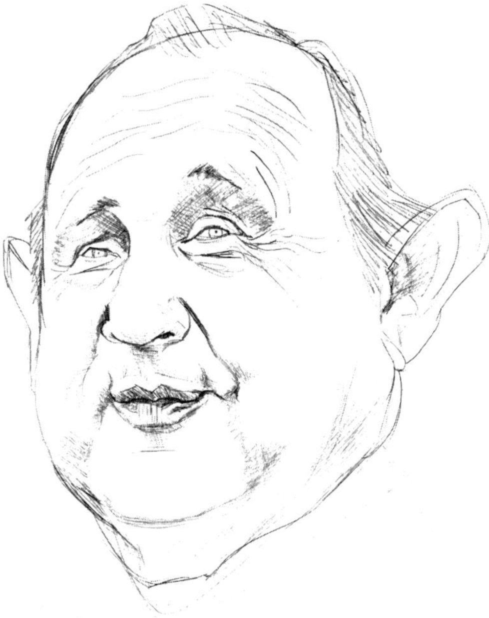

West Germany's minister for foreign affairs, Hans-Dietrich Genscher, and Chancellor Helmut Kohl have joined a coalition. Both of them have strongly supported the placement of nuclear missiles in West Germany.

Laurel and Hardy were waiting for Genscher and Kohl. I'm just sorry that Genscher isn't skinny. Genscher was to wear the big pants, which hold both of them. The original photo from a film was so foggy that I had to use my own models in order to reproduce the scene from the beginning. I tried to keep as close as possible to the original.

Here come Laurel and Hardy spraying nuclear deodorant all over.

I wonder what has made this piece so popular. Is it because people recognize Laurel and Hardy, or is it because of nuclear fear, or is it just because Genscher and Kohl look so ridiculous?

CHARLIE CHAPLIN

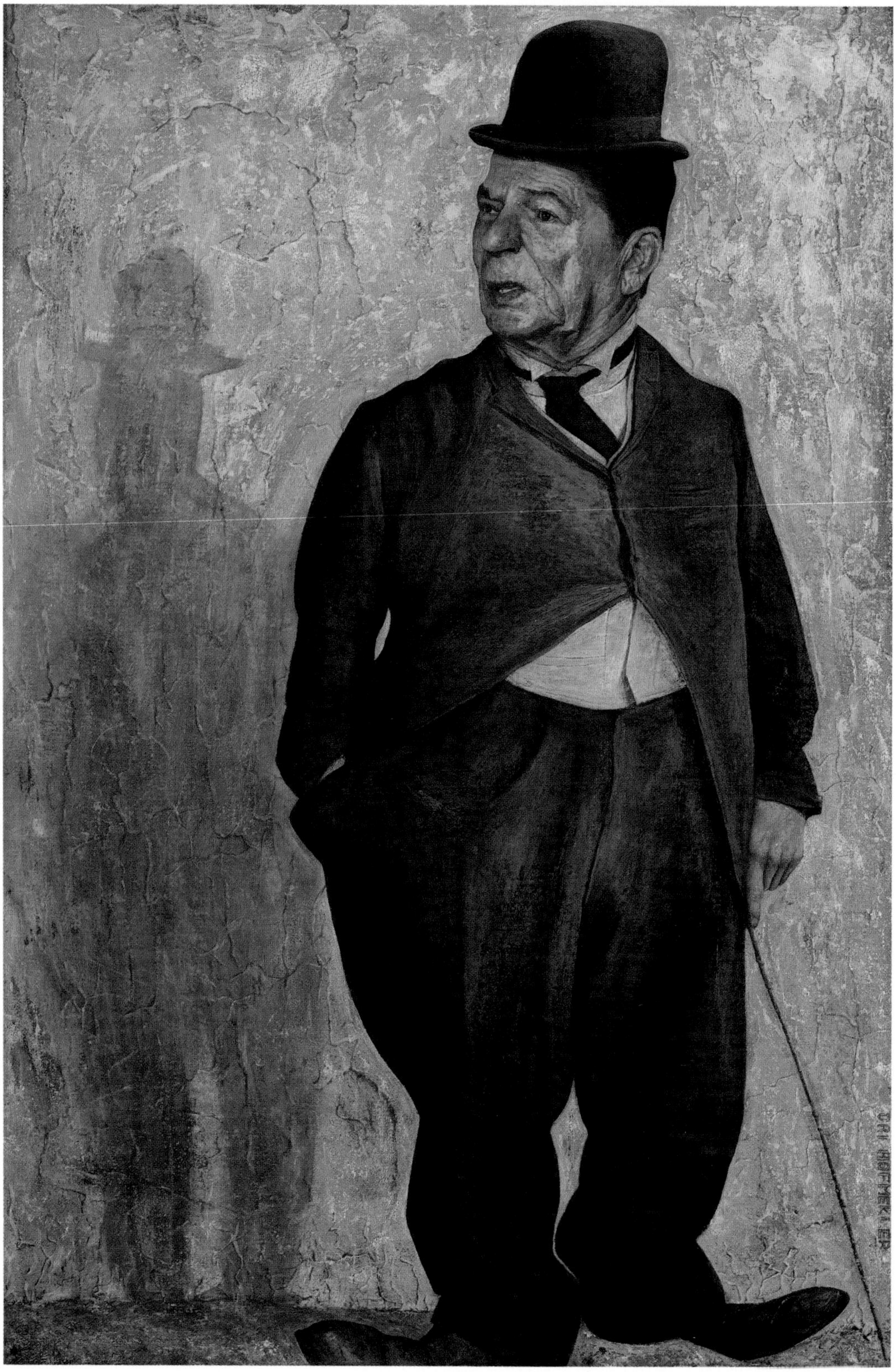

RONALD REAGAN, PRESIDENT OF THE UNITED STATES

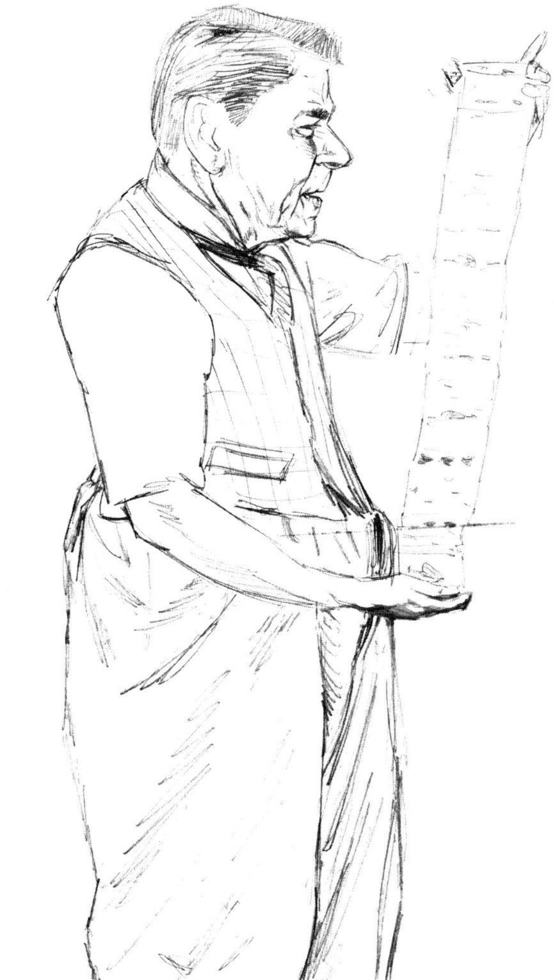

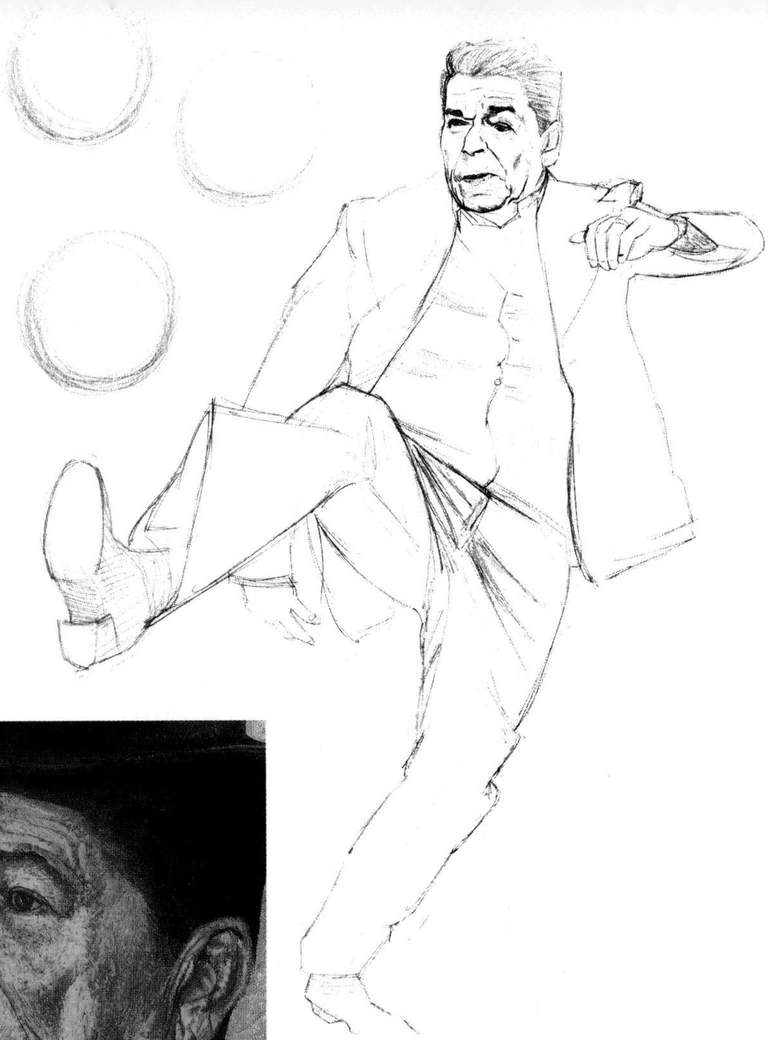

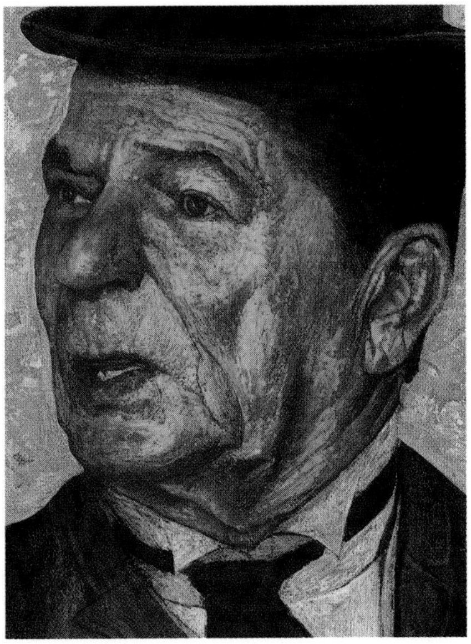

The Chaplin piece was done just before the 1980 presidential election. I knew that Reagan had been in show biz, and I remembered a Chaplin quote that goes something like "We comedians belong to almost the lowest level of society, which is just one level above politicians." That's more or less what I think, even if Chaplin didn't say it exactly like that.

I just wanted to point out that Reagan could be a comedian president, which is a little different from just being president.

Moreover, I planned it like this:

(1) If Reagan won the election, then it would be a comedian who turned the presidency into show biz.

(2) If Reagan lost the election, then I would call the picture "The End," like the famous "The End" of Charlie Chaplin's movies.

If Reagan does not change the Constitution by the 1988 election so he can run again, I will be able to use the second option as well.

THE GREAT DICTATOR

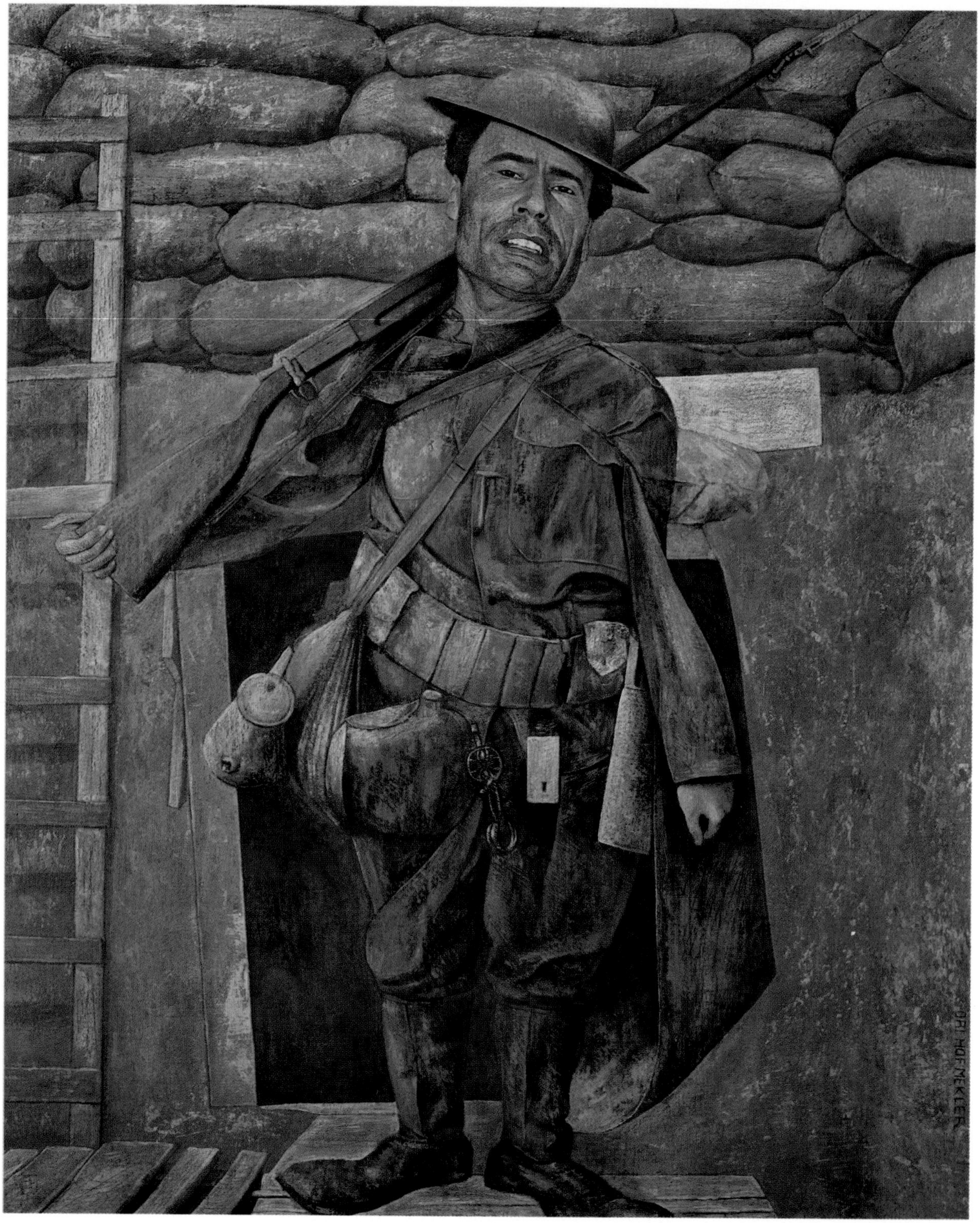
ORI HOFMEKLER

MUAMMAR QADDAFI, PRESIDENT OF LIBYA

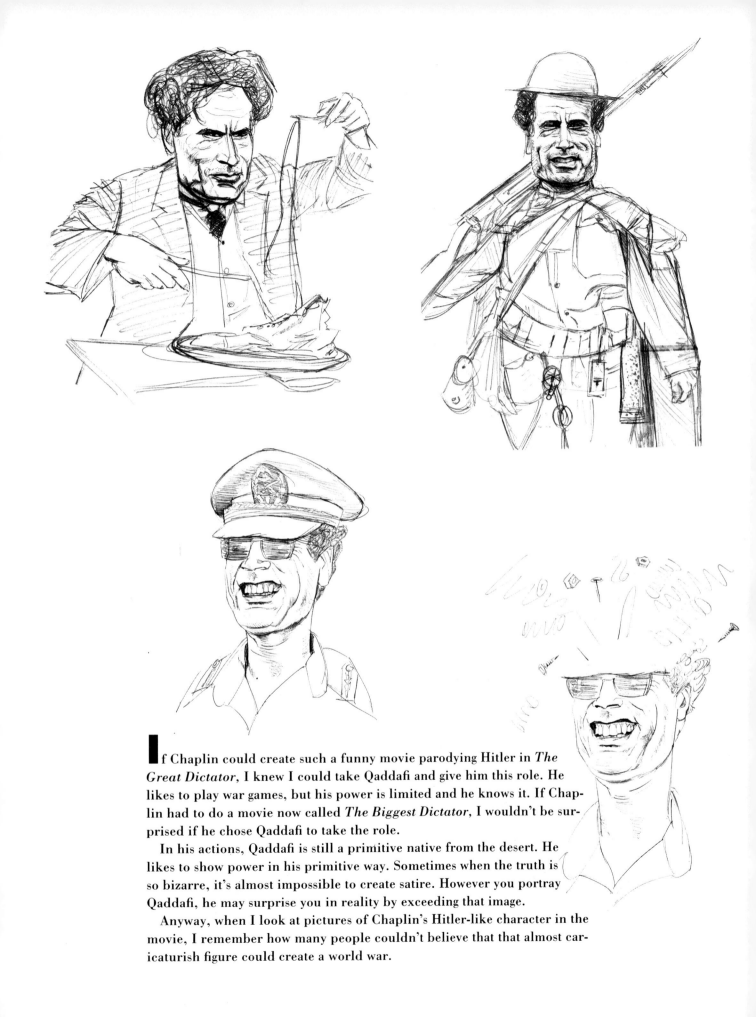

If Chaplin could create such a funny movie parodying Hitler in *The Great Dictator*, I knew I could take Qaddafi and give him this role. He likes to play war games, but his power is limited and he knows it. If Chaplin had to do a movie now called *The Biggest Dictator*, I wouldn't be surprised if he chose Qaddafi to take the role.

In his actions, Qaddafi is still a primitive native from the desert. He likes to show power in his primitive way. Sometimes when the truth is so bizarre, it's almost impossible to create satire. However you portray Qaddafi, he may surprise you in reality by exceeding that image.

Anyway, when I look at pictures of Chaplin's Hitler-like character in the movie, I remember how many people couldn't believe that that almost caricaturish figure could create a world war.

SHOW BIZ

BOY GEORGE BUSH AND THE VULTURE CLUB

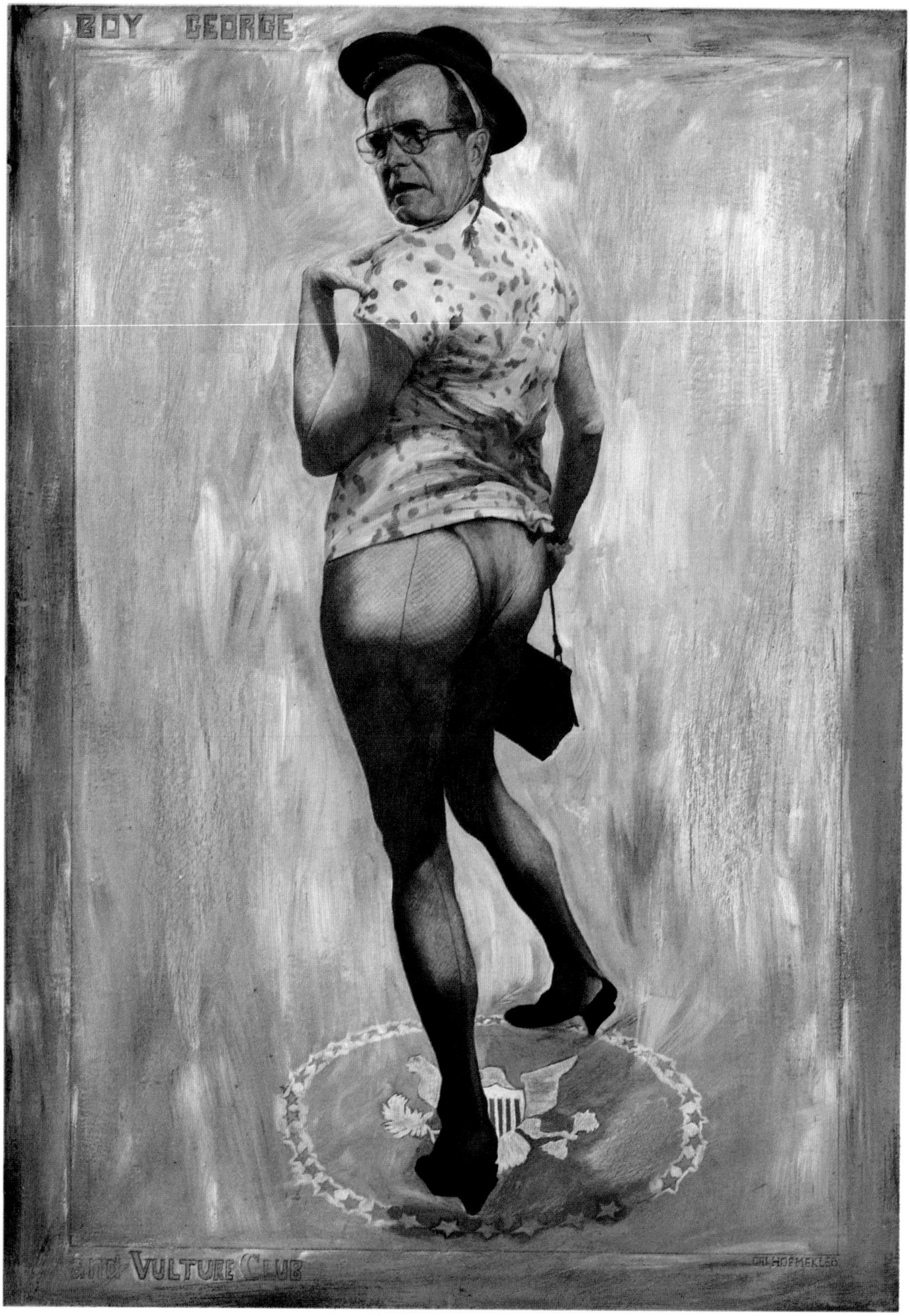
BOY GEORGE
THE VULTURE CLUB

GEORGE BUSH,
VICE PRESIDENT OF THE UNITED STATES

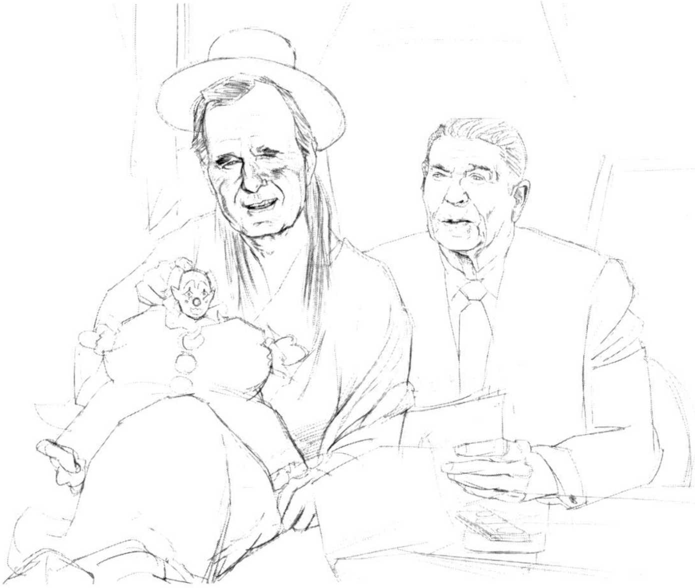

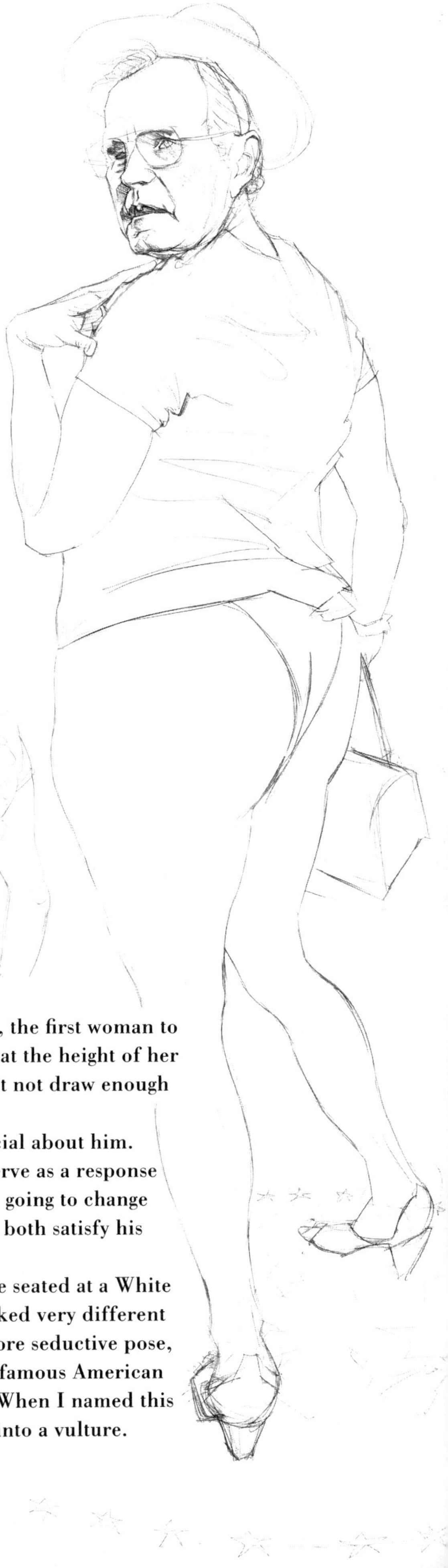

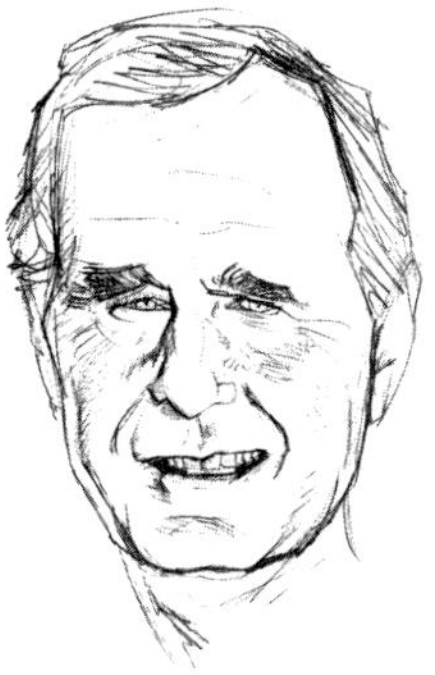

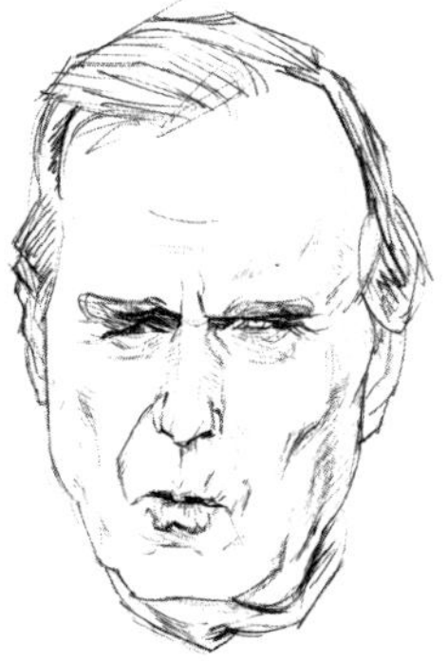

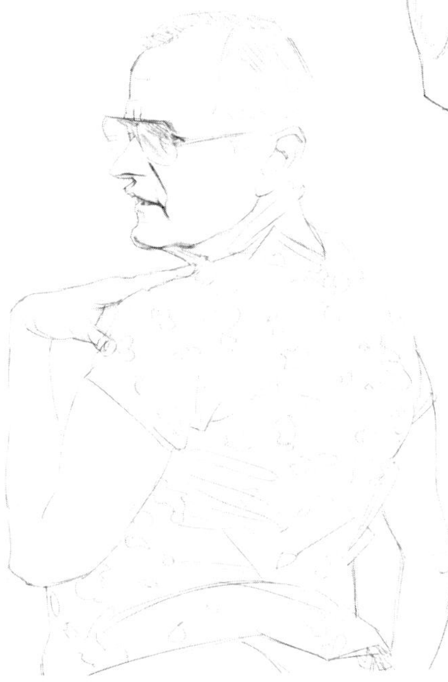

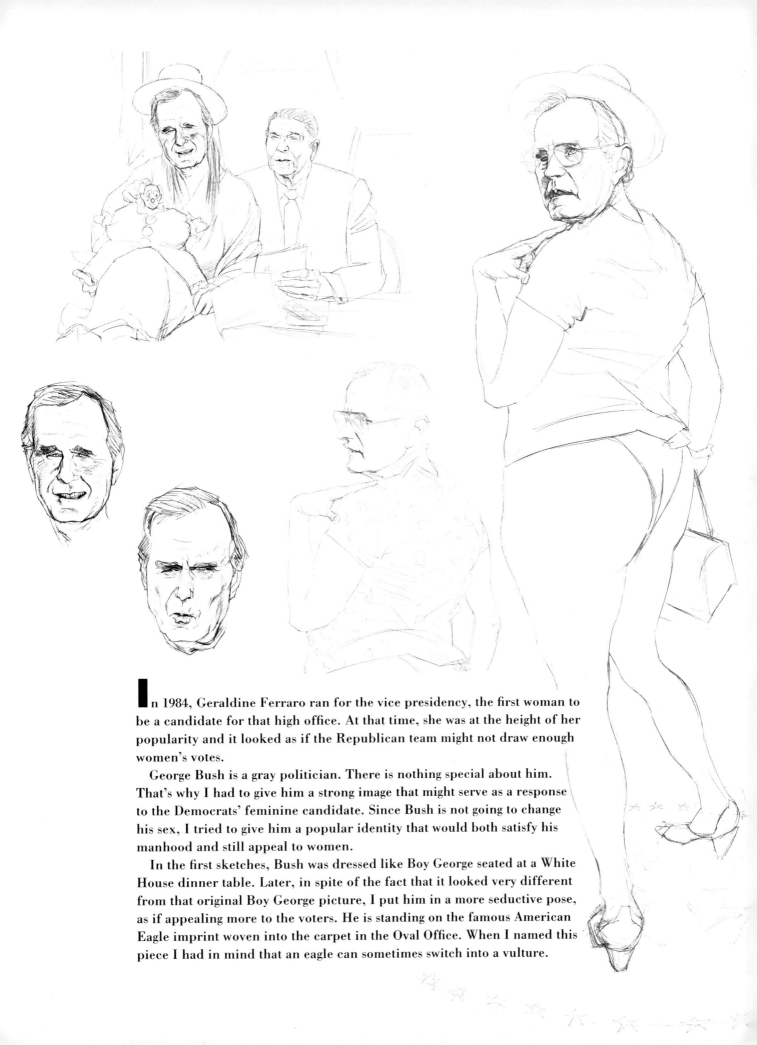

In 1984, Geraldine Ferraro ran for the vice presidency, the first woman to be a candidate for that high office. At that time, she was at the height of her popularity and it looked as if the Republican team might not draw enough women's votes.

George Bush is a gray politician. There is nothing special about him. That's why I had to give him a strong image that might serve as a response to the Democrats' feminine candidate. Since Bush is not going to change his sex, I tried to give him a popular identity that would both satisfy his manhood and still appeal to women.

In the first sketches, Bush was dressed like Boy George seated at a White House dinner table. Later, in spite of the fact that it looked very different from that original Boy George picture, I put him in a more seductive pose, as if appealing more to the voters. He is standing on the famous American Eagle imprint woven into the carpet in the Oval Office. When I named this piece I had in mind that an eagle can sometimes switch into a vulture.

BORN IN THE U.S.A.

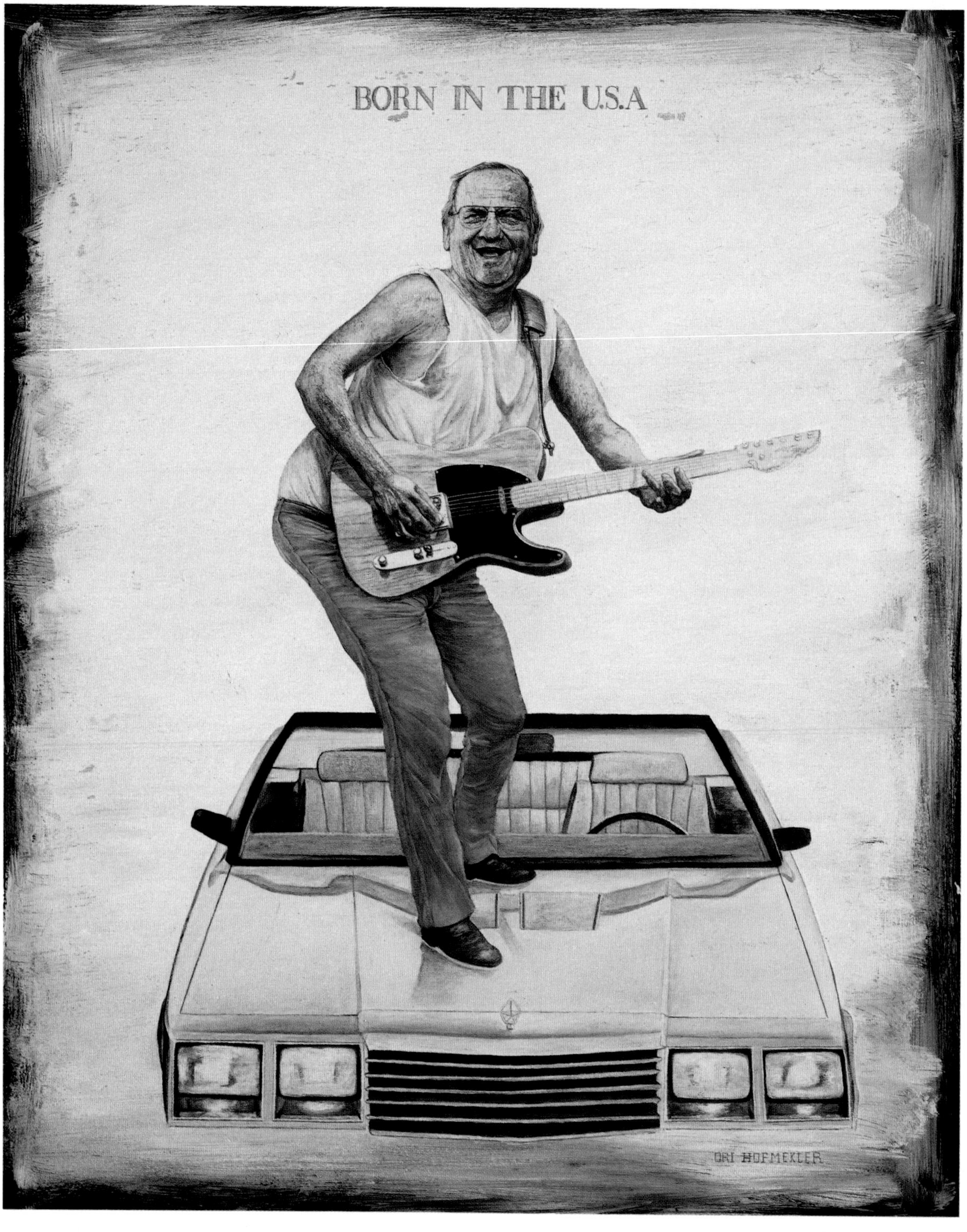
BORN IN THE U.S.A
ORI HOFMEKLER

LEE IACOCCA,
CHAIRMAN OF THE CHRYSLER CORPORATION

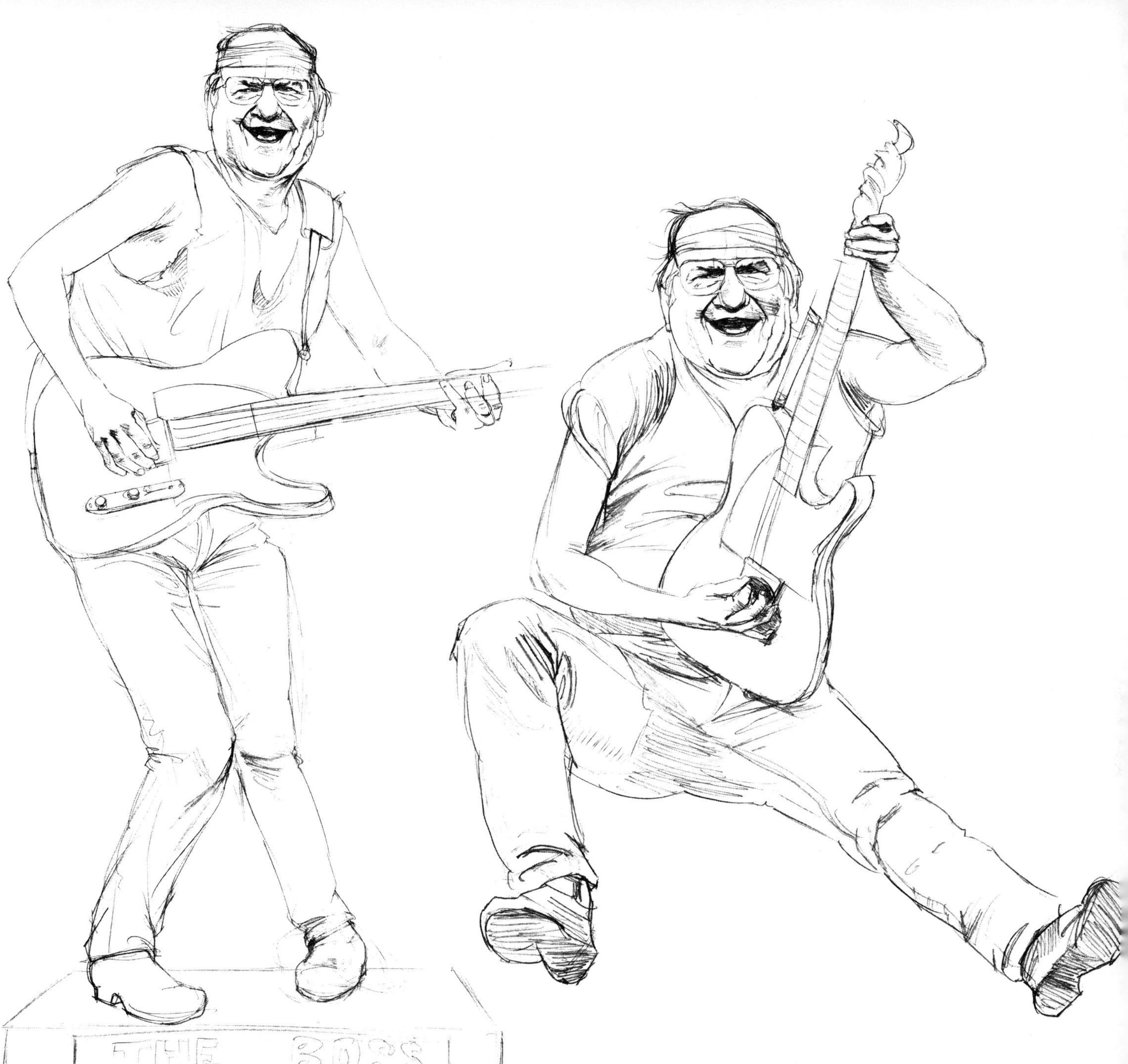
THE BOSS

Iacocca is a best-seller. In spite of the fact that he suffers adversity again and again, he rises up. America loves him.

Iacocca is full of PR. Everything he does is obvious. Iacocca sells cars, uses his image to sell cars, and runs for president all at the same time.

When the Chrysler boss used an imitation of Springsteen's "Born in the U.S.A." for a commercial, I gave him the chance to be the original. Here he stands on a Chrysler LeBaron, imitating the Boss. It suggests the following formula: politician = car salesman + show biz.

This is reality. There is no place for satire here.

HAROLD LLOYD

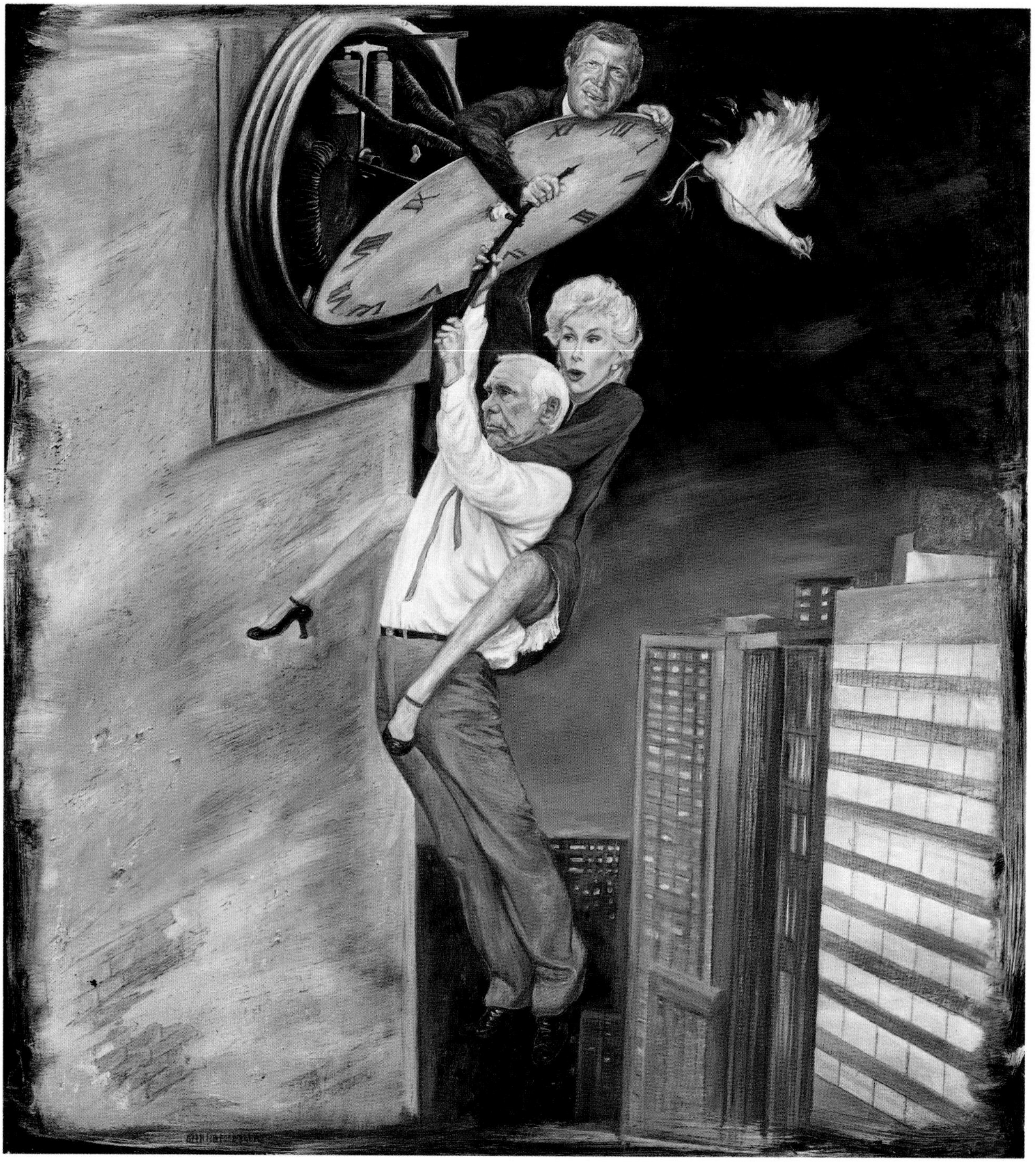

JOHNNY CARSON, DAVID LETTERMAN,
AND JOAN RIVERS, TV PERSONALITIES

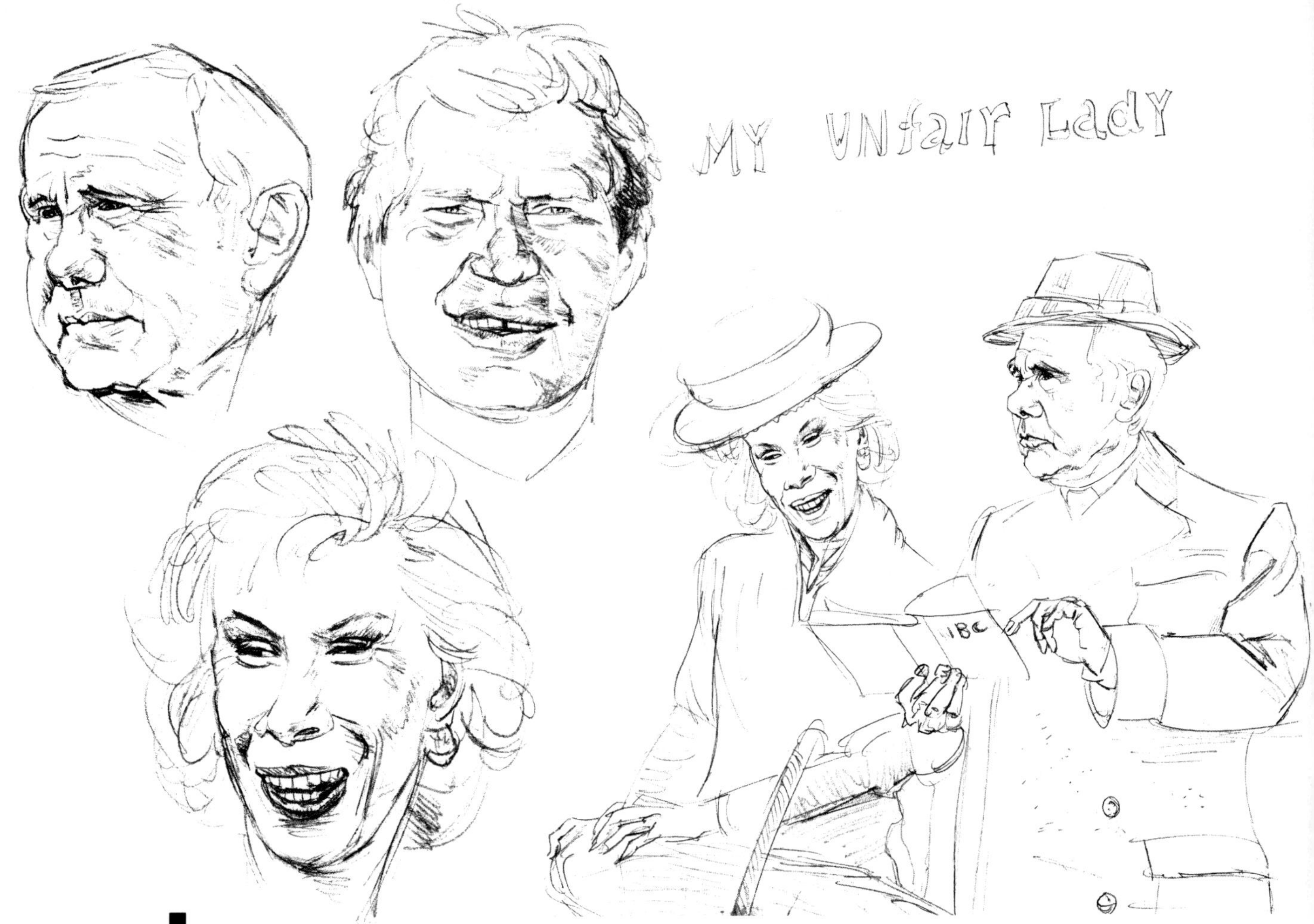
MY UNFAIR LADY
IBC

I've been waiting a long time for the opportunity to portray Johnny Carson. Carson is a clown, and I need perfect timing and the perfect situation to satirize a clown well.

The competition that sprang up between late-night talk-show hosts Carson and Joan Rivers and comparisons with David Letterman gave me the opportunity to deal with the talk-show king. Who is really on top of late-night television, and who is going to fall off or literally run out of time. That's what led me to this famous Harold Lloyd clock scene.

I tried a few ideas, and almost went for My Unfair Lady. Actually, Letterman didn't figure in it at all until the end, when I realized the scene didn't make sense without the host of the hottest late-night program in America at that moment.

Letterman brings a particularly unusual assortment of guests and pets to his show. For him, anyone is good enough as long as he or she (or it) is fun. Significantly, part of his routine consists of throwing things from high places. I needed someone to put the lid on the other two, to give their fight some perspective, and Letterman and his chicken clock high above the city took care of that perfectly.

Carson and Rivers are both trying to hold on, at the same time, to the favorable time slot, and to me seem ironically doomed by this struggle to kill each other off. Letterman is already "safe," controlling another slot altogether. But despite all the activity, by the look of the empty, quiet city background, you can see that America really couldn't care less about this struggle—it has already gone to sleep.

STEREOTYPES

LOUIS XV

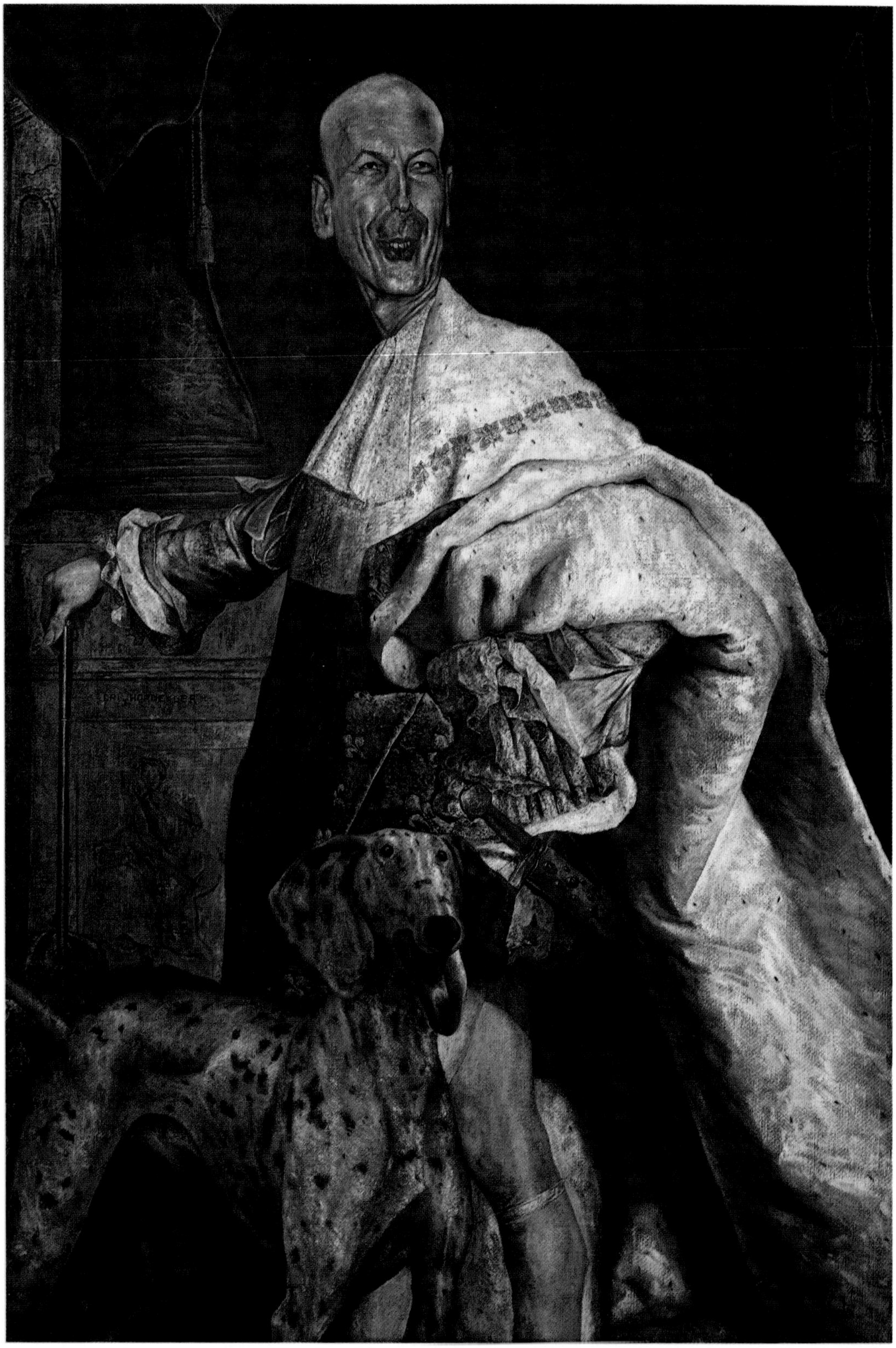

VALÉRY GISCARD D'ESTAING,
FORMER PRESIDENT OF FRANCE

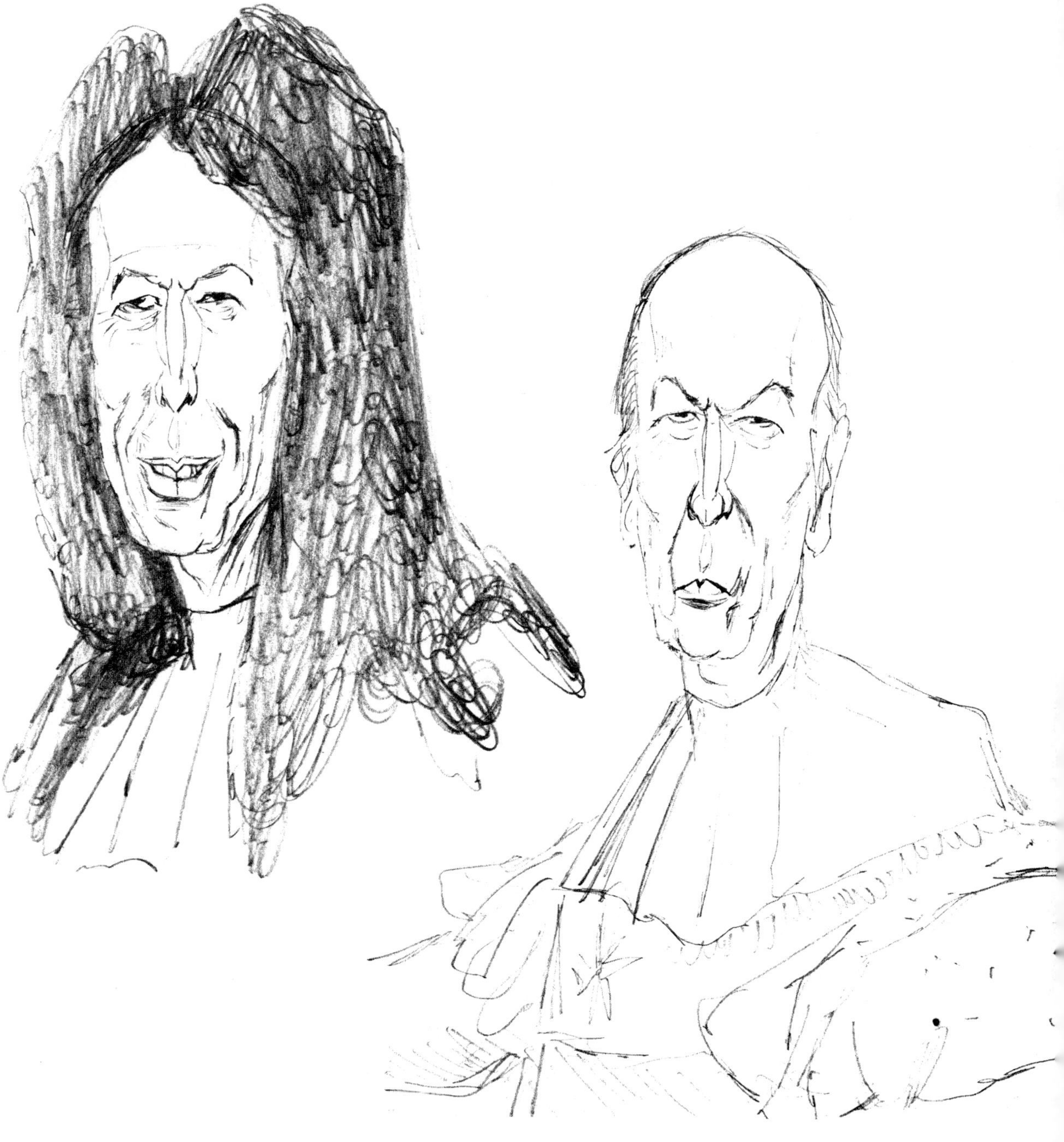

I don't know why, but while I was sketching this piece, the only words that jumped into my mind were "Et tu, Valéry?"

Giscard truly believes that he is a descendant of Louis XV. Here he is taking the role of Louis XIV, who was at least the most "visual" French monarch. Anyway, who cares if it is Louis XIV or Louis XV as long as His Majesty, Giscard, is actually king?

Giscard appeals to the sentimental belief of his people, their need for a patriarch. The king in France took absolute power. That becomes an ideal for any politician in power in France.

I personally don't understand why someone wants so much to be a king. I would find it so unpleasant to be dressed like that.

THE GODFATHER

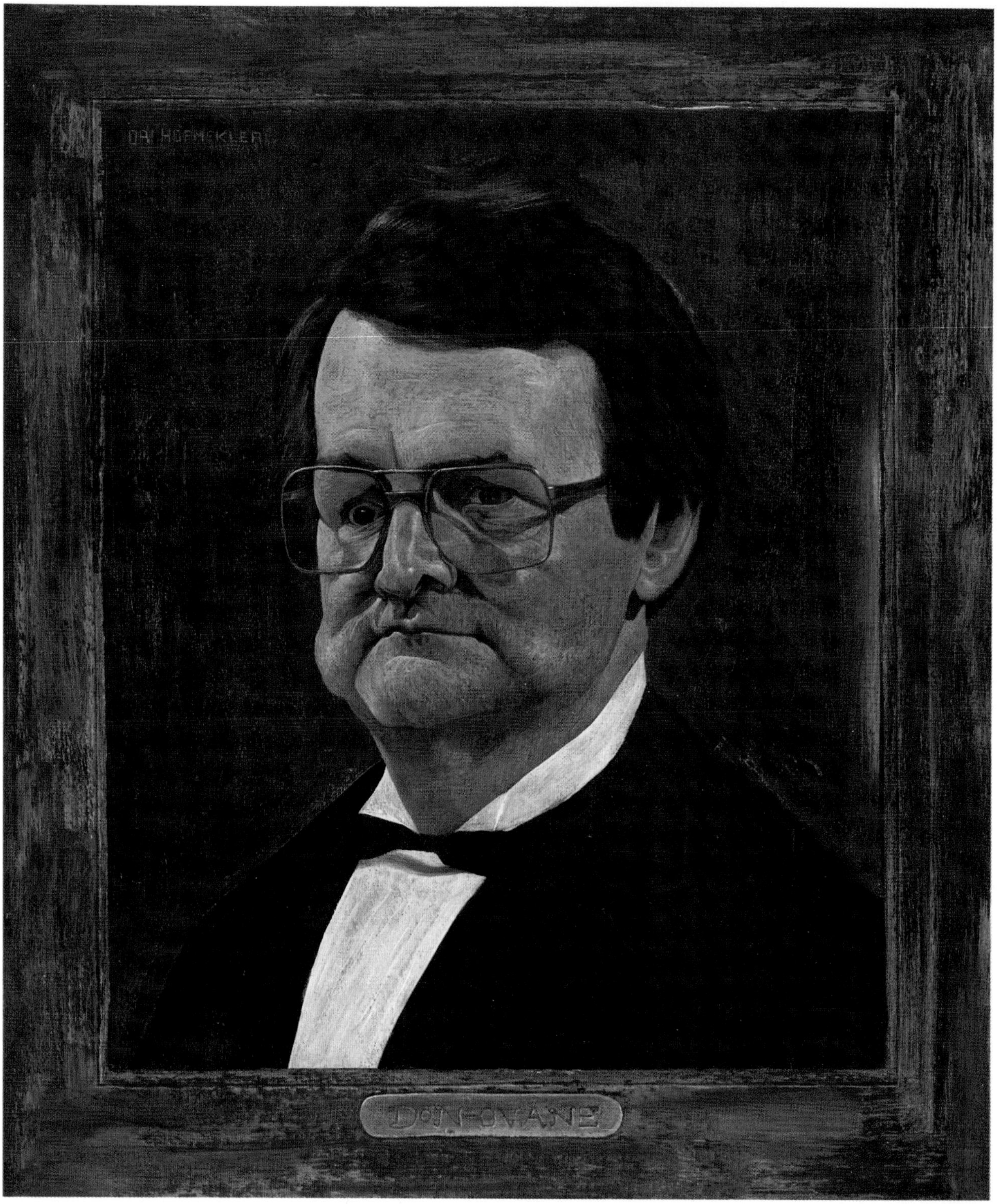

DONOVANE

RAYMOND J. DONOVAN,
FORMER U.S. SECRETARY OF LABOR

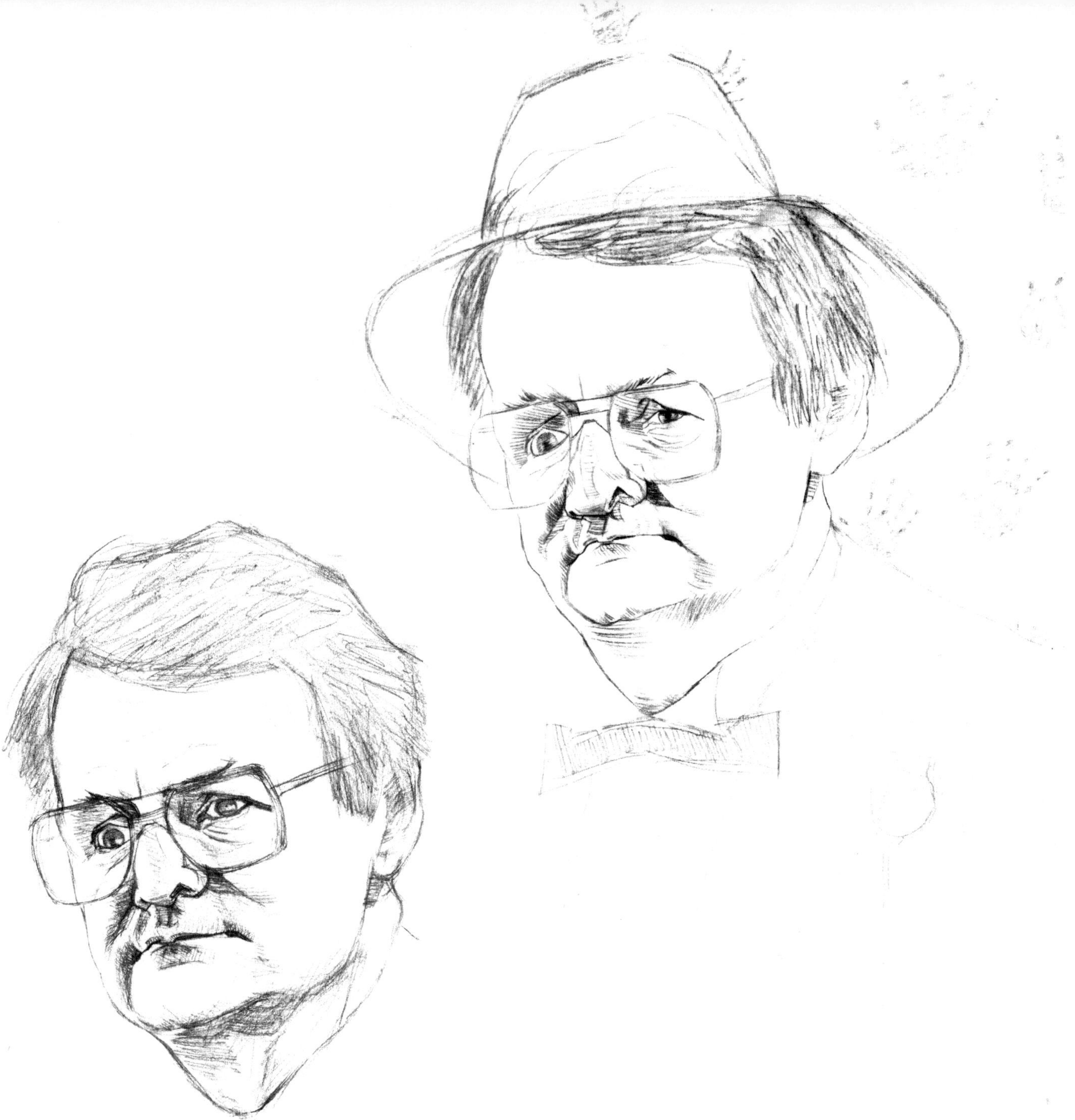

The Donovan piece was commissioned by *Rolling Stone* magazine. I drew it in the middle of the Raymond Donovan scandal. I put him in the role of The Godfather, Don Corleone, pumped up his cheeks and called him Don Novane.

At that time *Rolling Stone* feared a lawsuit over the title, which had a Mafia connotation. So they printed my picture with the title cut off.

I was annoyed that my picture didn't appear the way I wanted it to.

A few years later, when Donovan was found "not innocent," I got to see this piece in its entirety on the cover of the *New Republic*.

EASY RIDER

POPE JOHN PAUL II

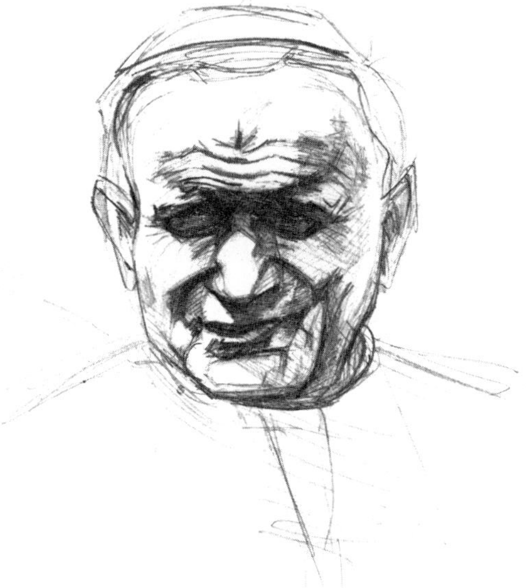

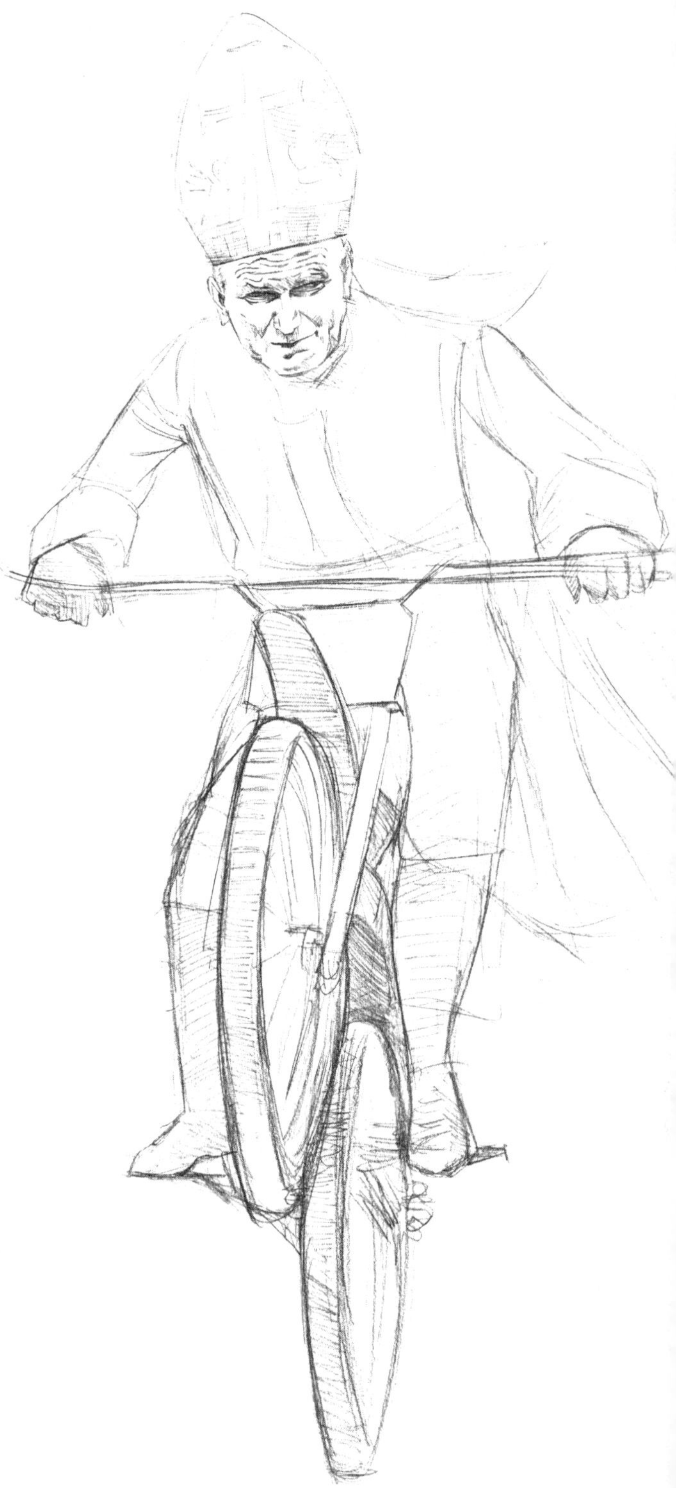
pop a wheely

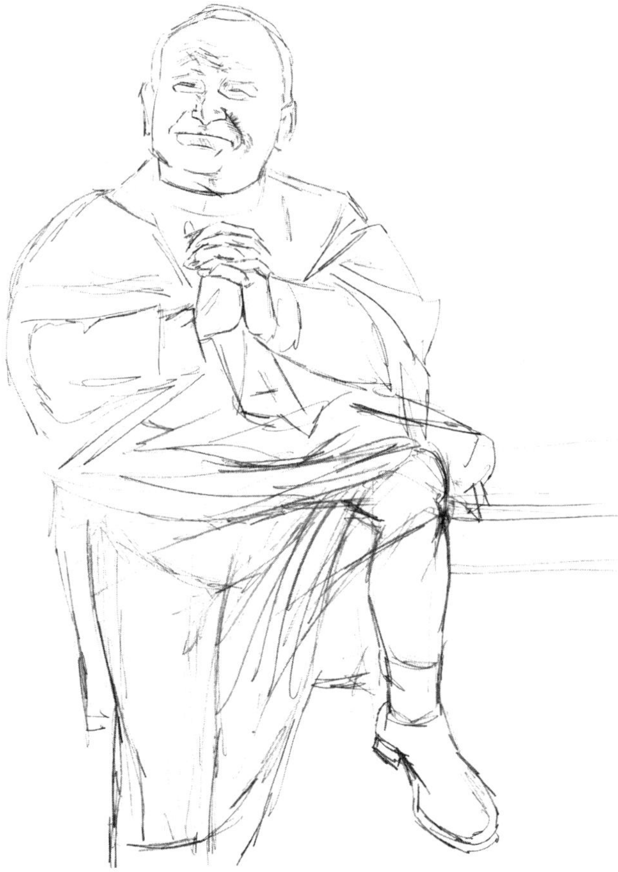

The Catholic pope is a symbol surrounded by a thousand years of tradition. Everything is old, old, old. This pope did something new. He is the most philosophical pope: he writes poetry, he talks to the Jews, he talks about ideas like freedom, he is indirectly involved in politics. He is very romantic, though his conservatism lingers on. All of these things together make him the "easiest" pope.

This pope is a hippie pope. He would have been a pope for the sixties, when the film *Easy Rider* spoke to a generation.

ABU SIMBEL

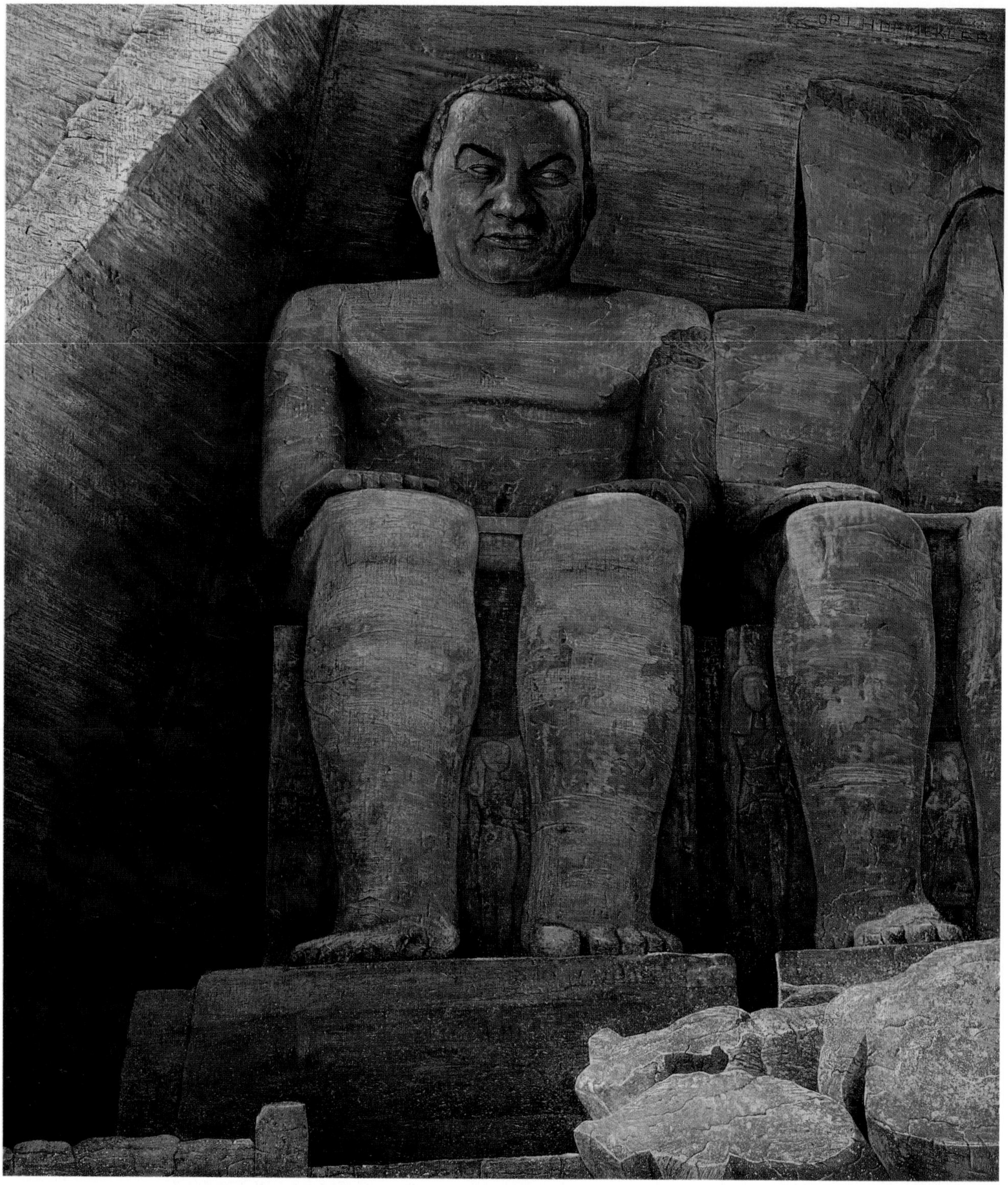

MUHAMMAD HOSNI MUBARAK, PRESIDENT OF EGYPT

Anwar Sadat was talkative, charming, very noisy. Hosni Mubarak is the opposite. His face reminds me of the Pharaoh statues: stiff, cool, secretive. I was luckier with Mubarak than with Sadat. If I had tried to put Sadat at Abu Simbel, the other statues wouldn't have been able to stand it—too noisy.

Abu Simbel shows the Egyptian heritage, with its ancient legacy of power. Egyptians believe that they are the only ancestors of the pharaohs. Hence, the connection. To be a leader in Egypt, it is not enough to be prime minister.

What if the pharaoh's curse is not just a fairy tale? As long as Mubarak stays still and frozen in my picture, nothing bad is going to happen.

CHILDREN'S SHOWS

THE QUEEN OF HATS

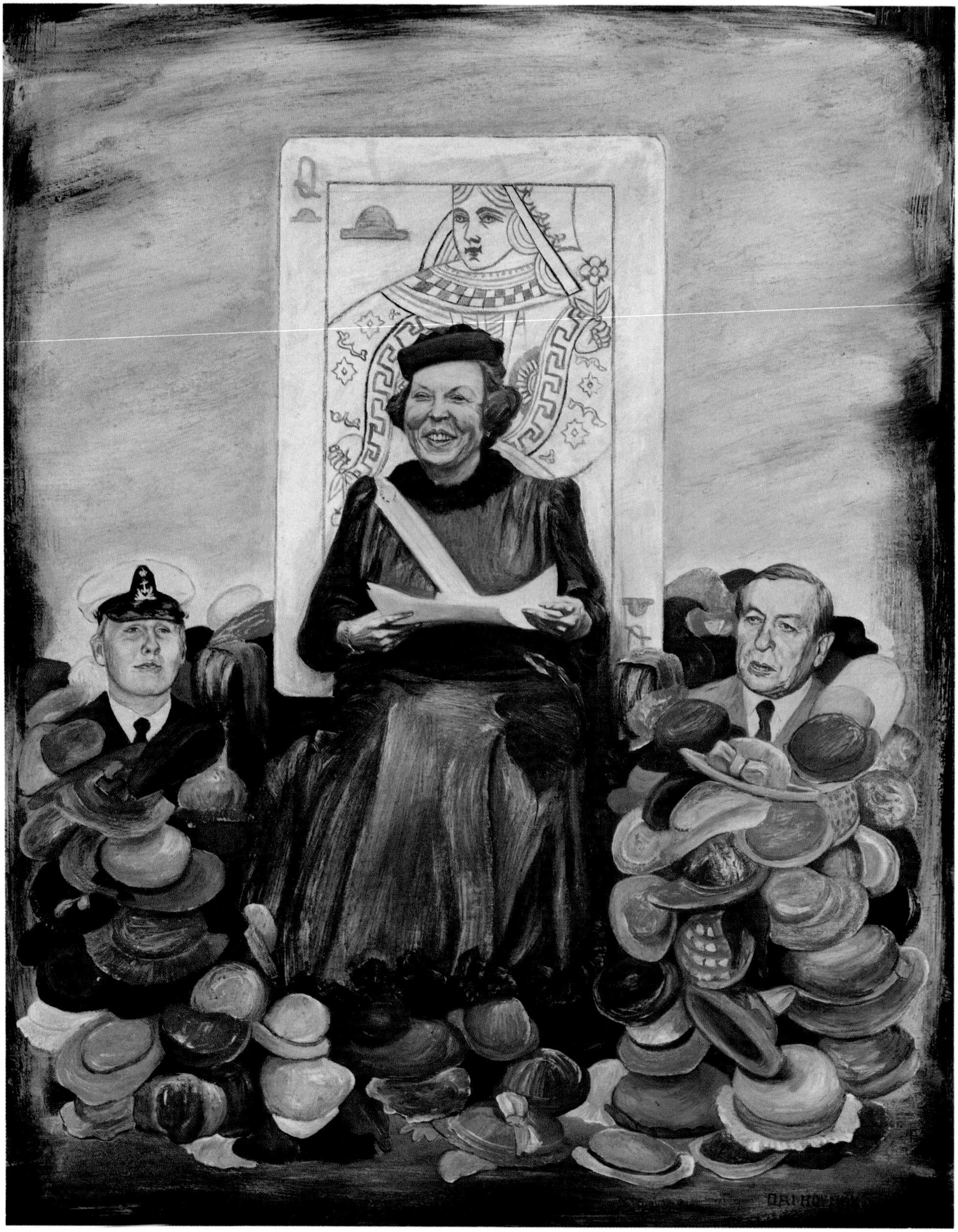

QUEEN BEATRIX OF THE NETHERLANDS

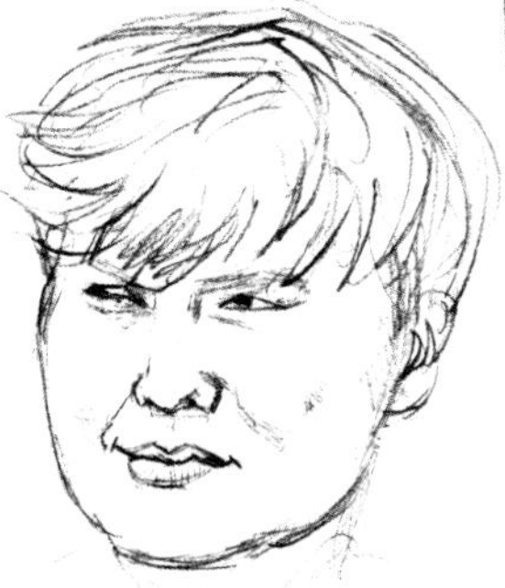

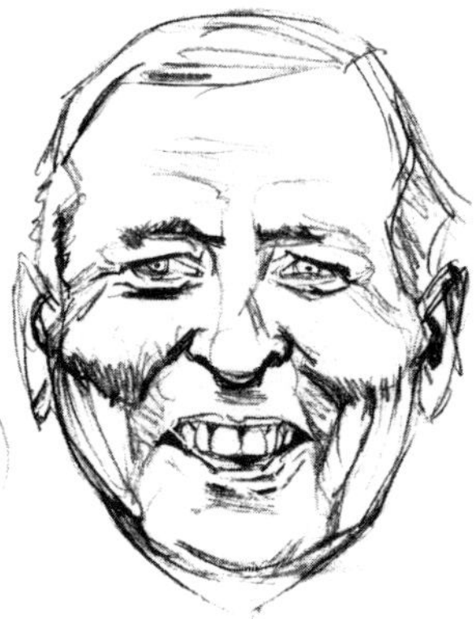

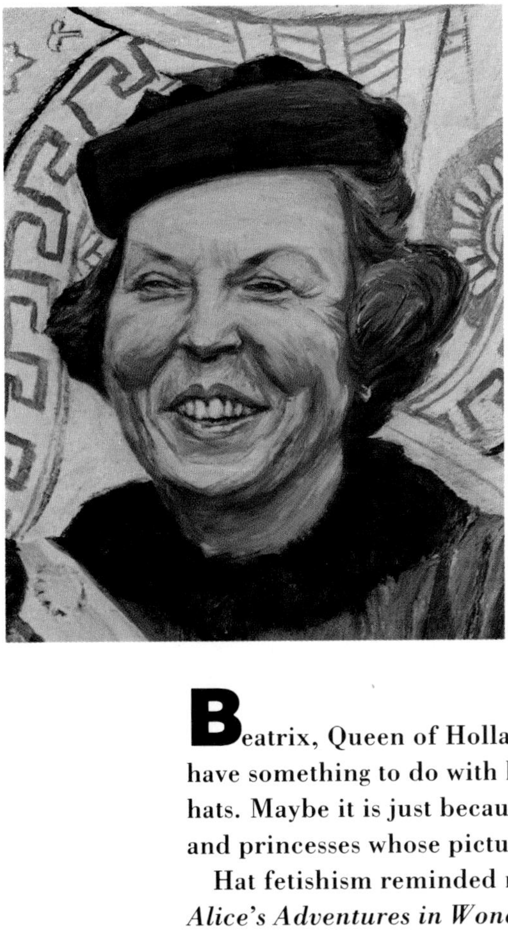

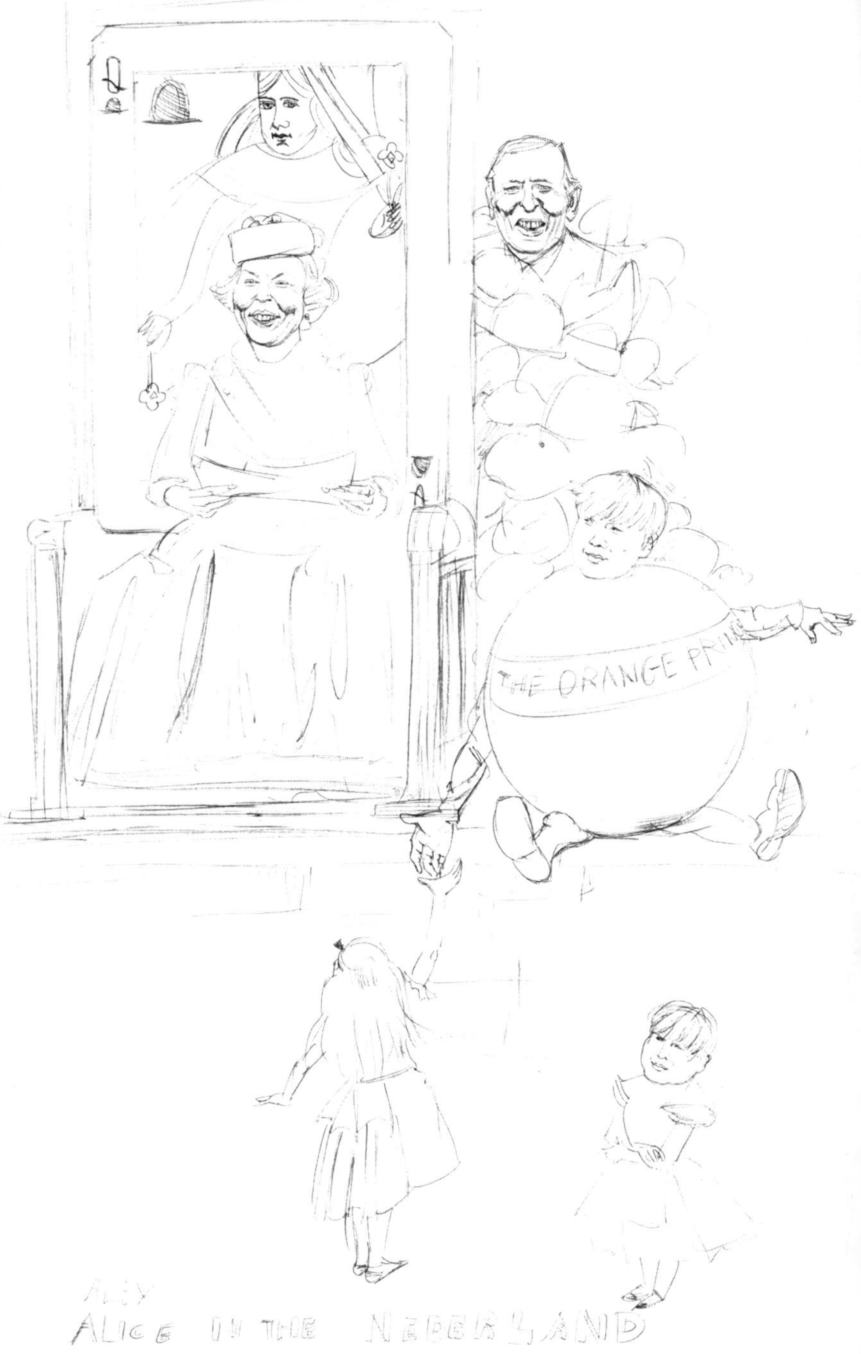
THE ORANGE
ALICE IN THE NEDERLAND

Beatrix, Queen of Holland, is a hat fetishist. It looks as if royal families have something to do with hat fetishism or at least a strong attraction to hats. Maybe it is just because most of the royalty today consists of queens and princesses whose pictures are taken a lot.

Hat fetishism reminded me of the Mad Hatter from Lewis Carroll's *Alice's Adventures in Wonderland.* Royalty always looked to me like part of a child's fairy tale. I tried some sketches on the Wonderland idea and later I moved to the subject with the Queen of Hats instead of the Queen of Hearts. Wonderland and the Netherlands are the same to me, so long as the Mad Hatter is the subject.

Royalty represents an excellent blood mixture that has to keep its unique quality from one generation to another. Unfortunately I wasn't born a prince. Maybe that's the reason I like to read fairy tales about kings, queens, princes, and princesses. Everything looks so clean, so life doesn't look that bad.

E.T. AND THE MIDGET EAST SOLUTION

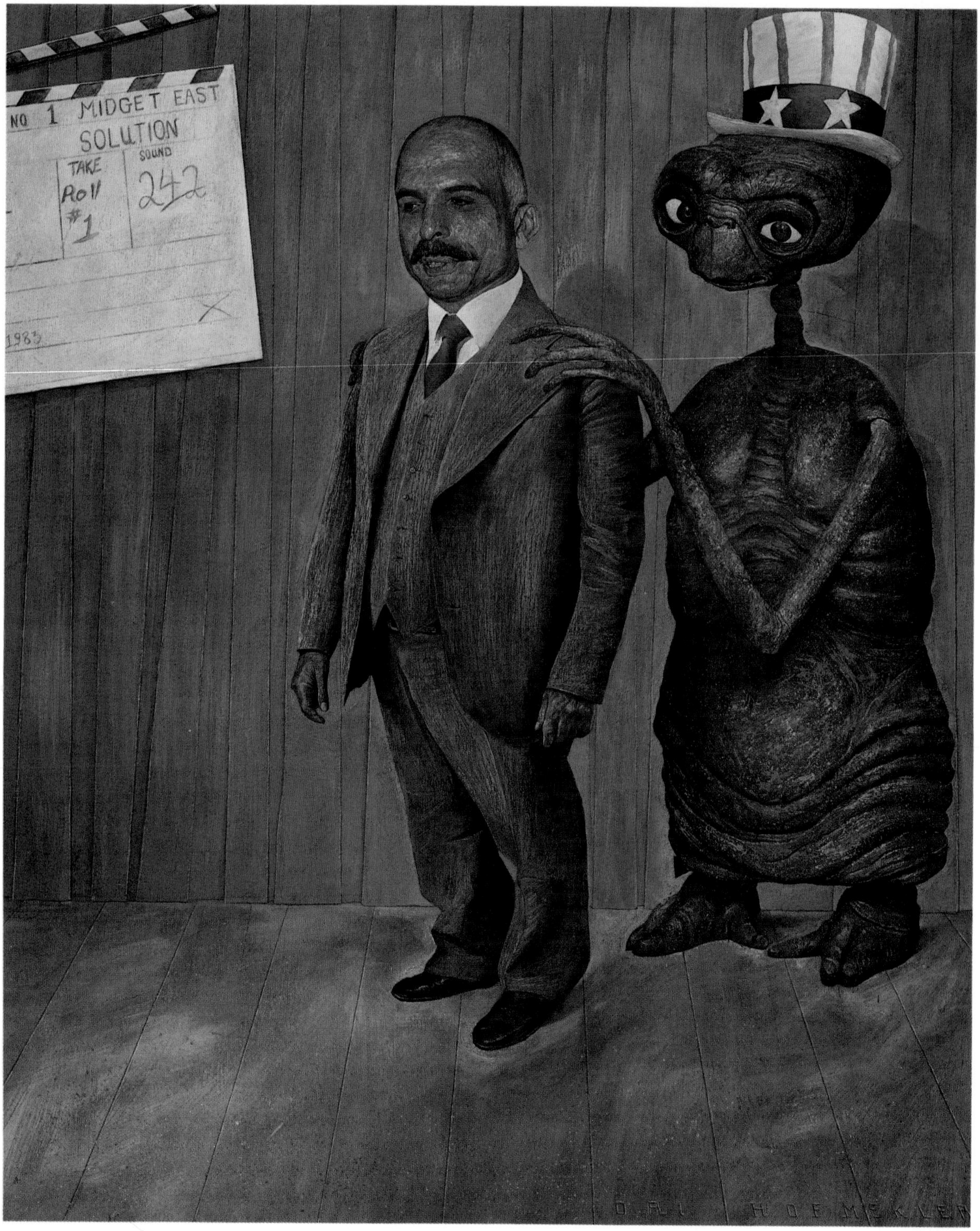
NO 1 MIDGET EAST
SOLUTION
TAKE
SOUND
Roll
#1
242
1983
DALI HOFMEKLER

E.T. AND KING HUSSEIN OF JORDAN

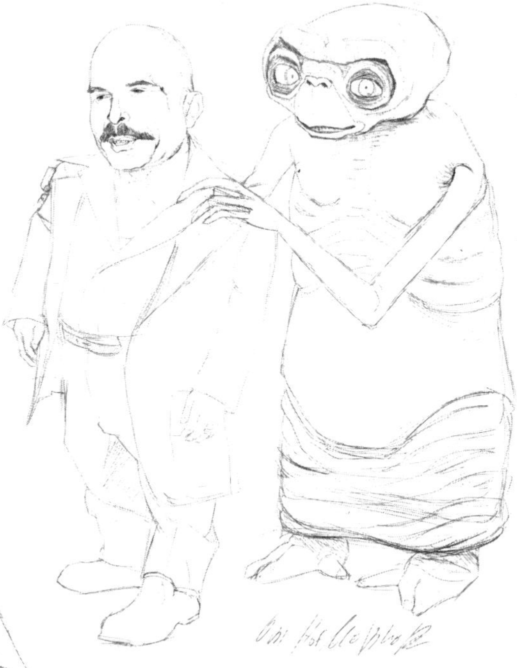

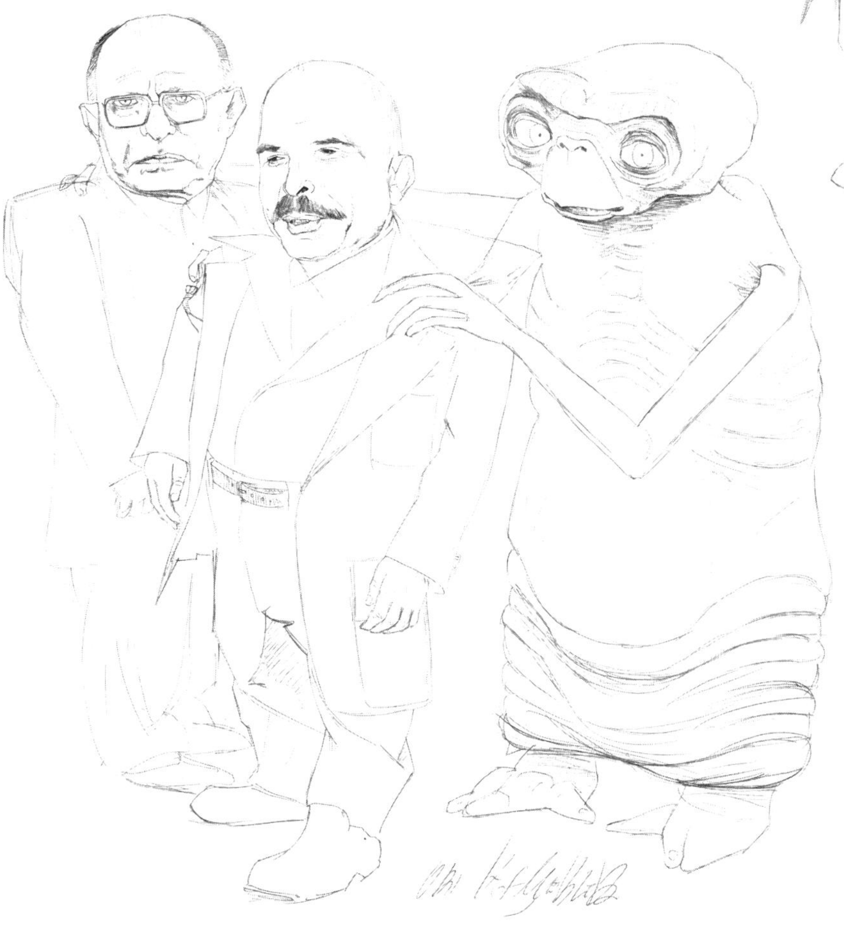

During the time when *E.T.* was the hottest movie, President Reagan was trying to plan a peaceful solution in the Middle East, using the rather diminutive King Hussein as a key.

Midgets were on top of everything in those days. I simply thought that the combination of King Hussein and E.T. might work and if not, maybe E.T. alone is the magic solution to a very complicated political situation.

Another reason for doing this picture was that my son Daniel had asked me for an E.T. picture. He was very happy with the result, and didn't even ask me who the little man with the mustache was.

MEESE PIGGY

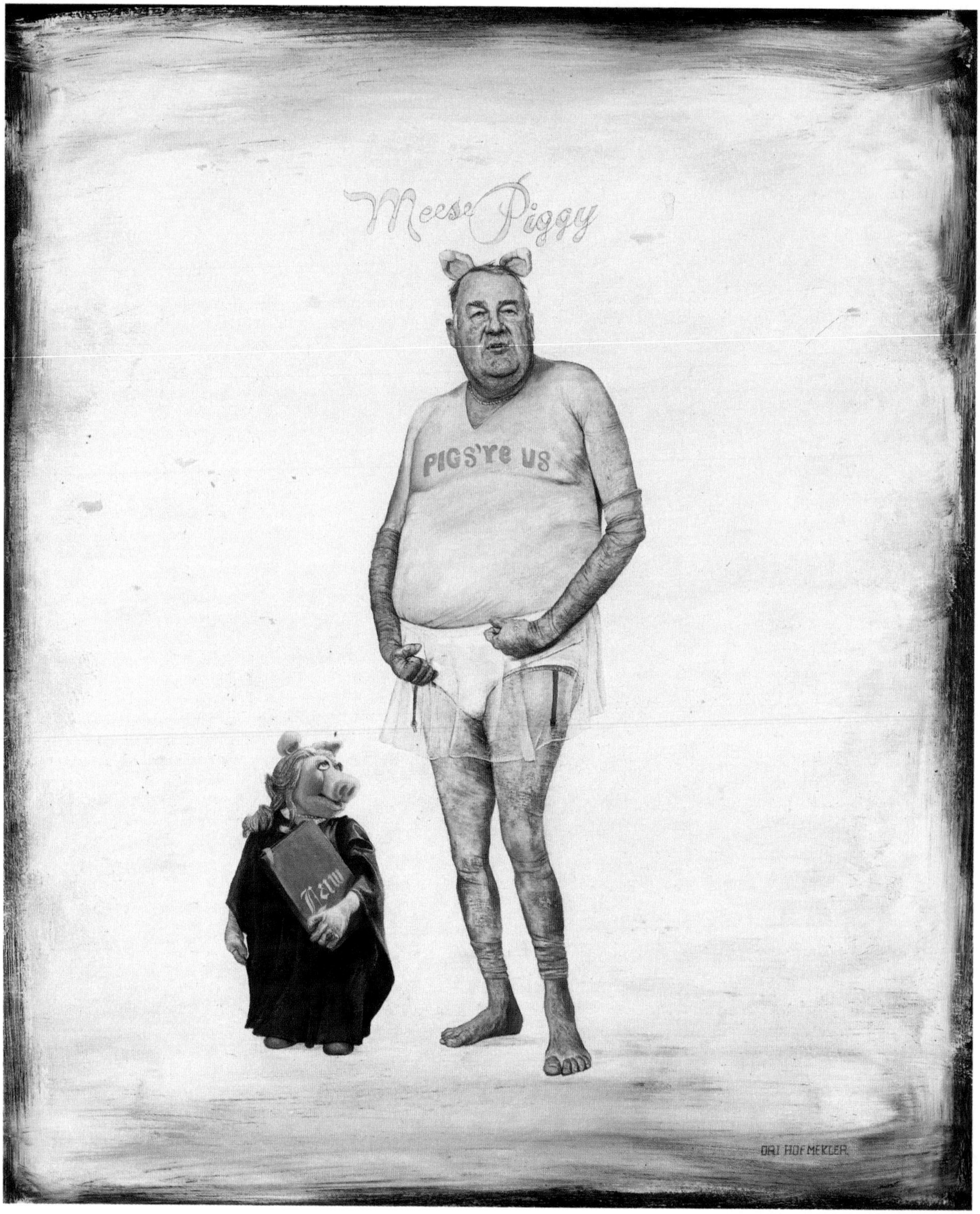
Meese Piggy
PIGS're US
ORI HOFMEKLER

EDWIN MEESE, U.S. ATTORNEY GENERAL

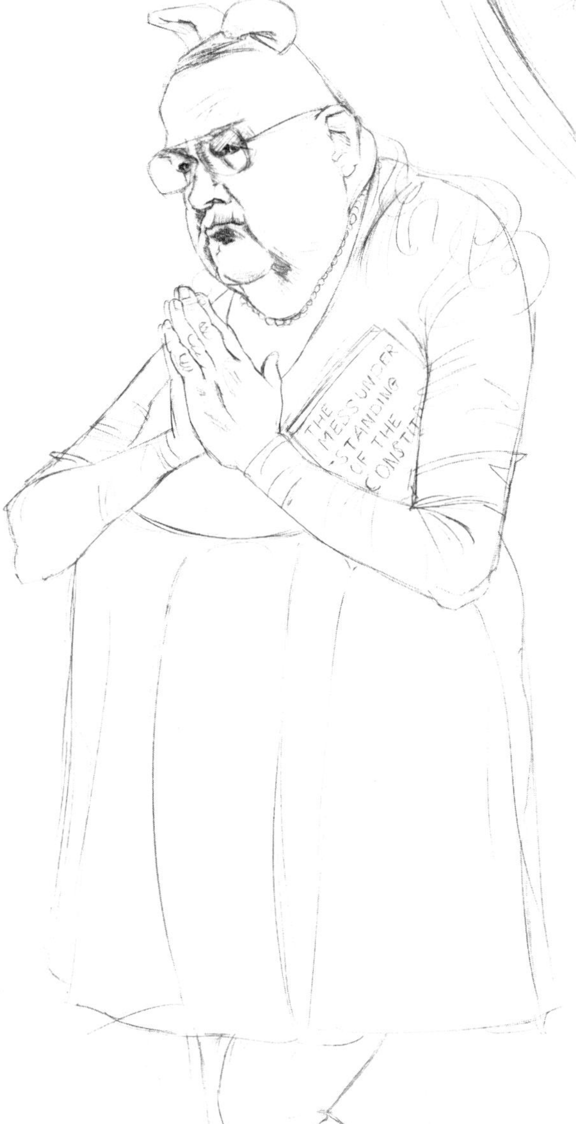
THE
MESSUNDER
STANDING
OF THE
CONSTIT

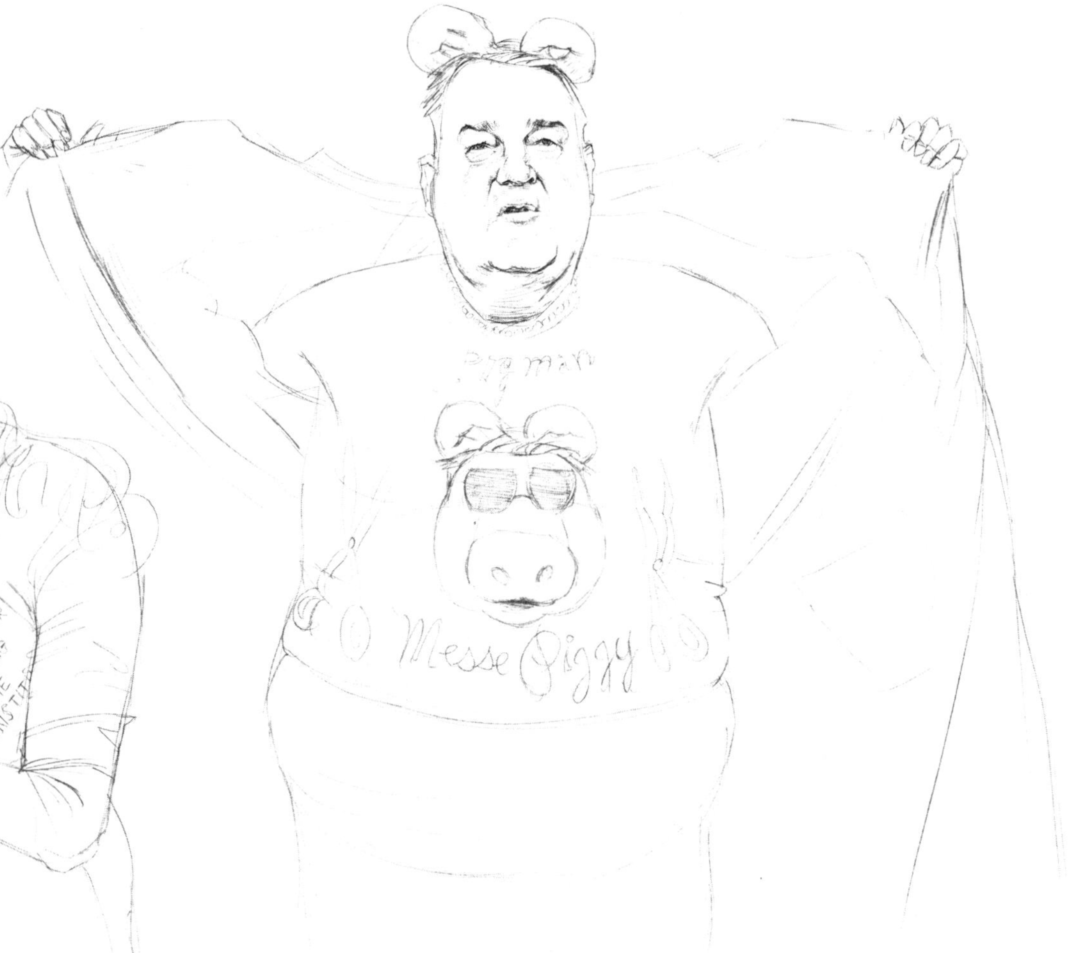
Messe Piggy

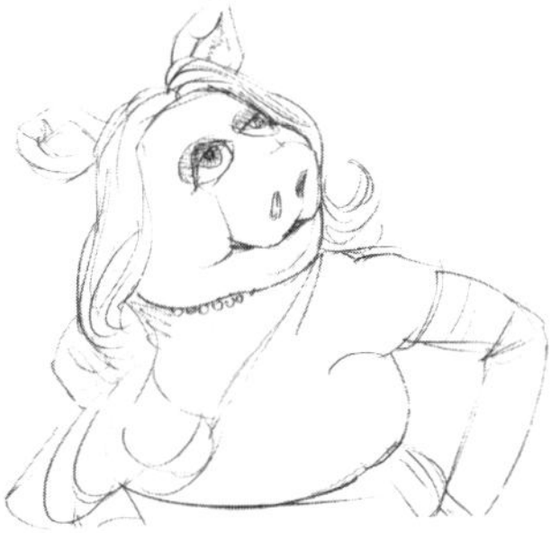

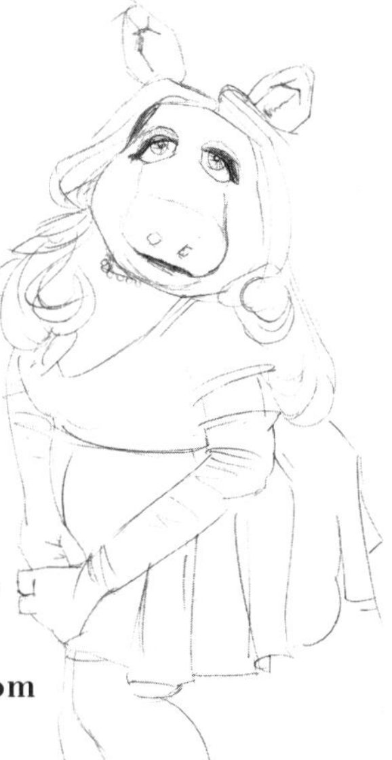

When Edwin Meese took command of the Commission on Pornography, I knew it was time for me to focus on him. From the first time I saw him at the White House I remembered his face.

The Commission's main aim was to keep the young generation away from obscenity. That's why I had to put Meese in a very nice children's show. Playing the role of Miss Piggy might give him a chance to be popular among the young generation, for whom he cares so much.

Just to make things even, Miss Piggy takes the attorney general's part.

TRADEMARKS

RONNIE WALKER

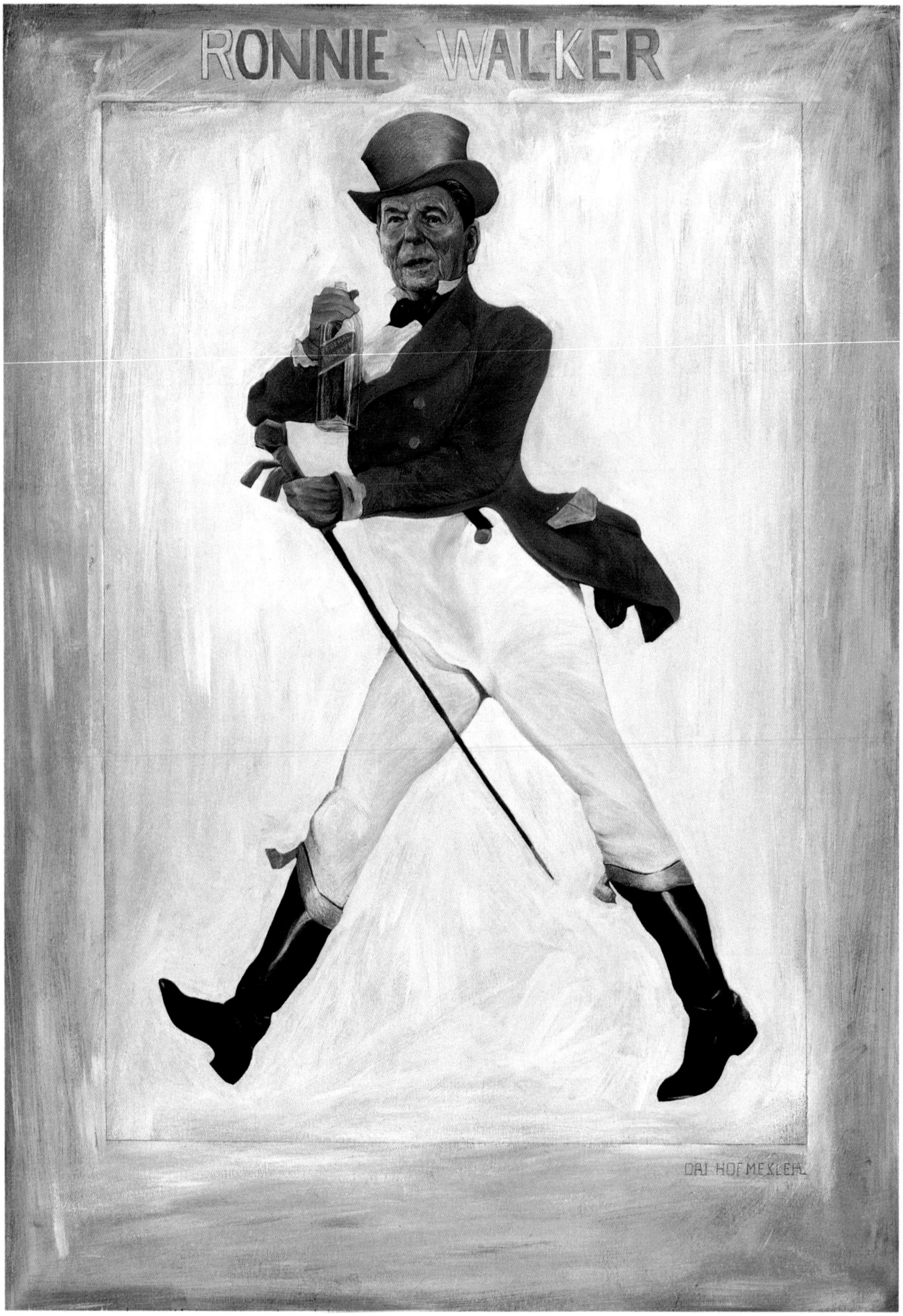
RONNIE WALKER
DAI HOFMEKLER

RONALD REAGAN, PRESIDENT OF THE UNITED STATES

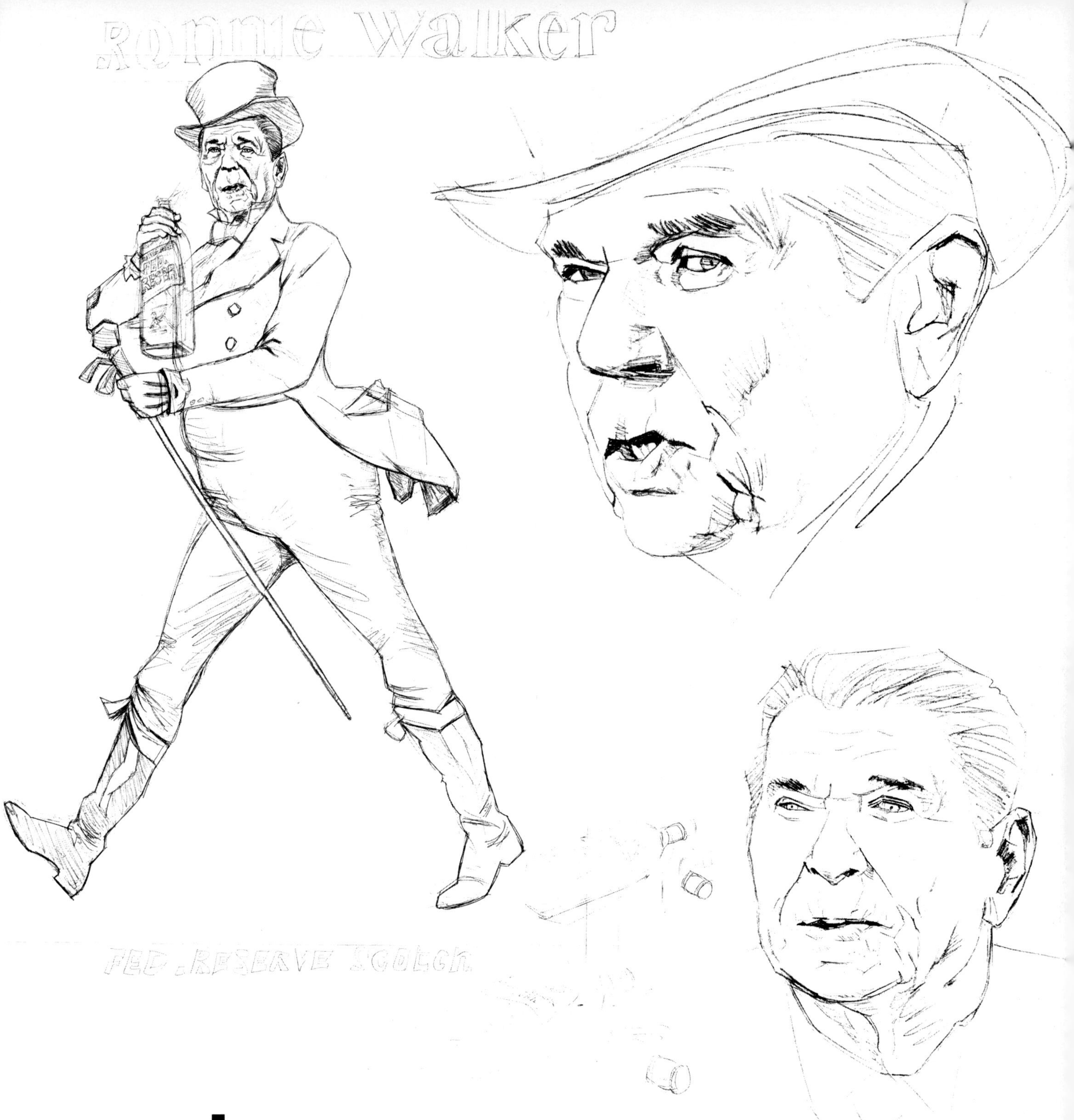
Ronnie Walker

Johnnie Walker was one of my best friends. He used to stand on my work table during the day. When I was under too much pressure, I noticed that Johnnie was almost always empty. It looked as if there was a permanent connection between pressure, Johnnie Walker, and a deficit (of liquor).

Realizing again and again that the bottle was empty gave me the idea to deal with another empty bottle—the bottle of the Federal Reserve. Here comes Ronnie Walker spending the Federal Reserve into the biggest deficit in history.

METRO GOLDWYN THATCHER

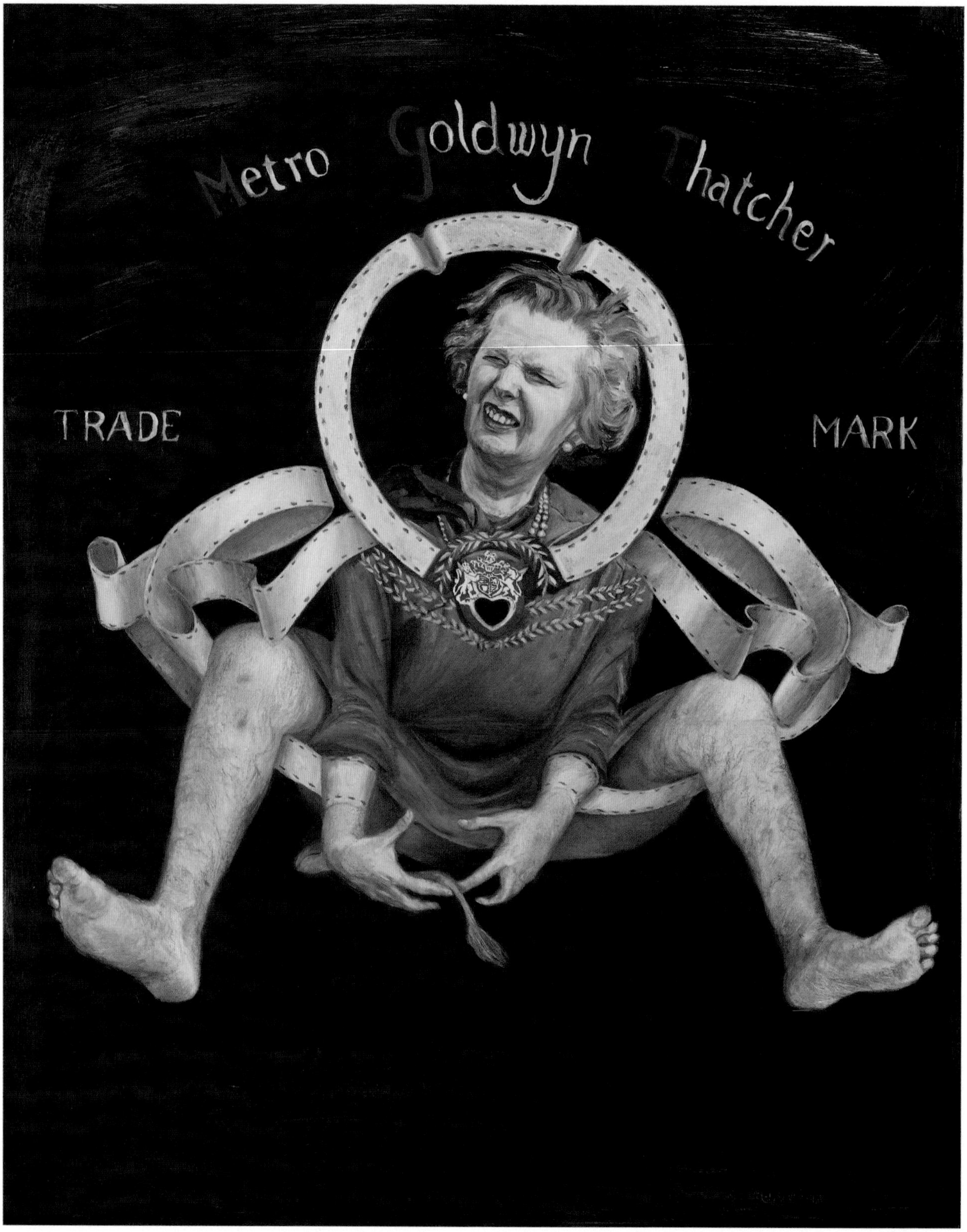

Metro Goldwyn Thatcher
TRADE
MARK

MARGARET THATCHER,
PRIME MINISTER OF GREAT BRITAIN

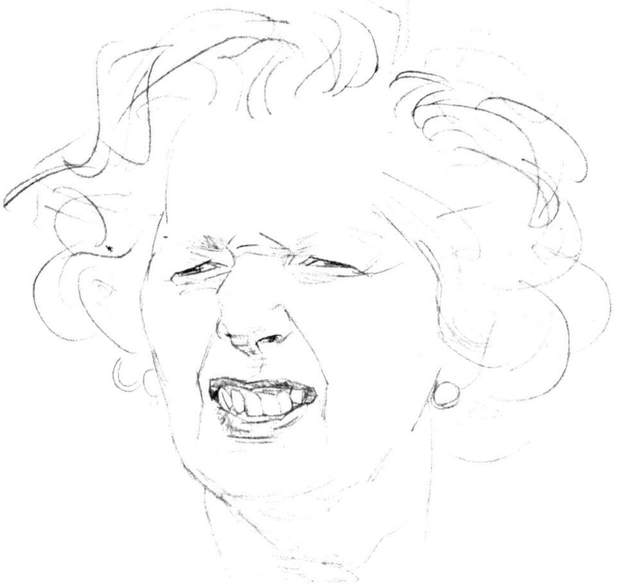

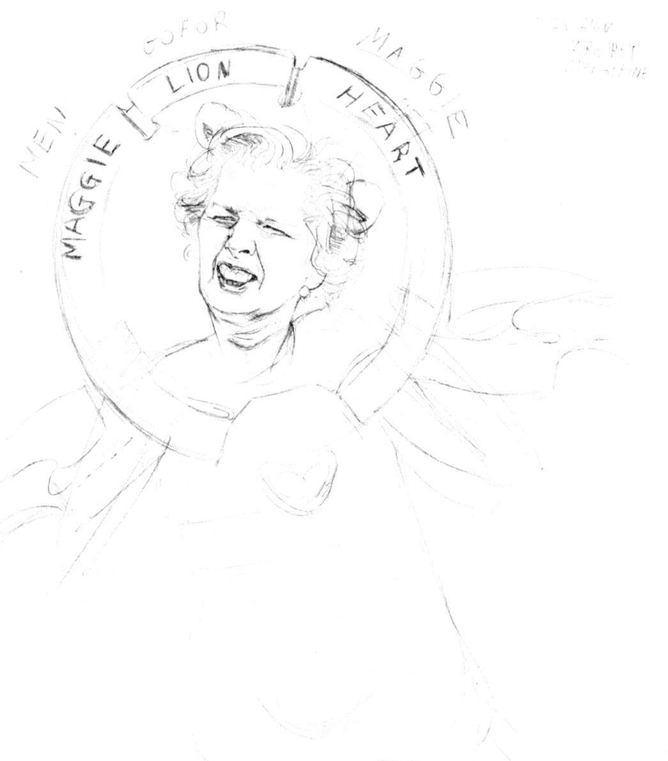
MEN
MAGGIE
LION
HEART
MAGGIE

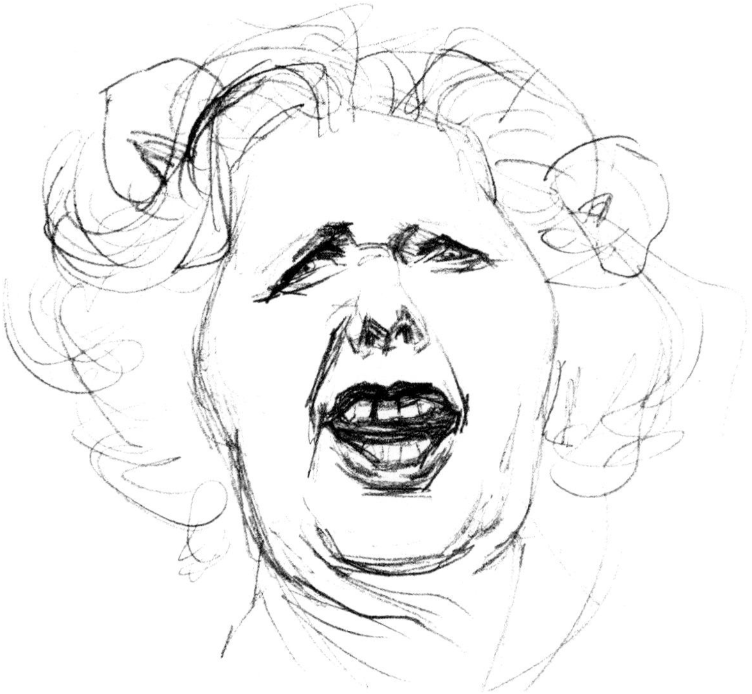

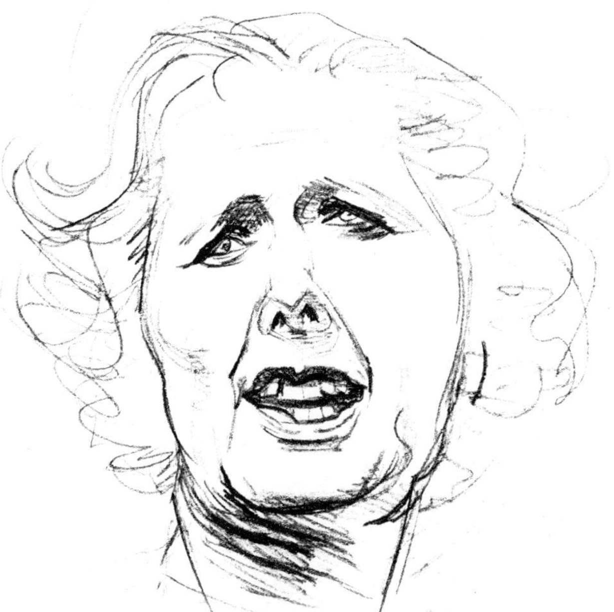

This is the case of a woman in power, Prime Minister Margaret Thatcher. Politics is based on power symbols. So is the show biz industry. Here is the British lion symbol and the MGM lion, with the prime minister in a way trapped between the two.

I deliberately kept her dressed because her clothes show part of her character. Anyway, all of this was just a big excuse to show her exciting legs.

THE THREE MONKEYS

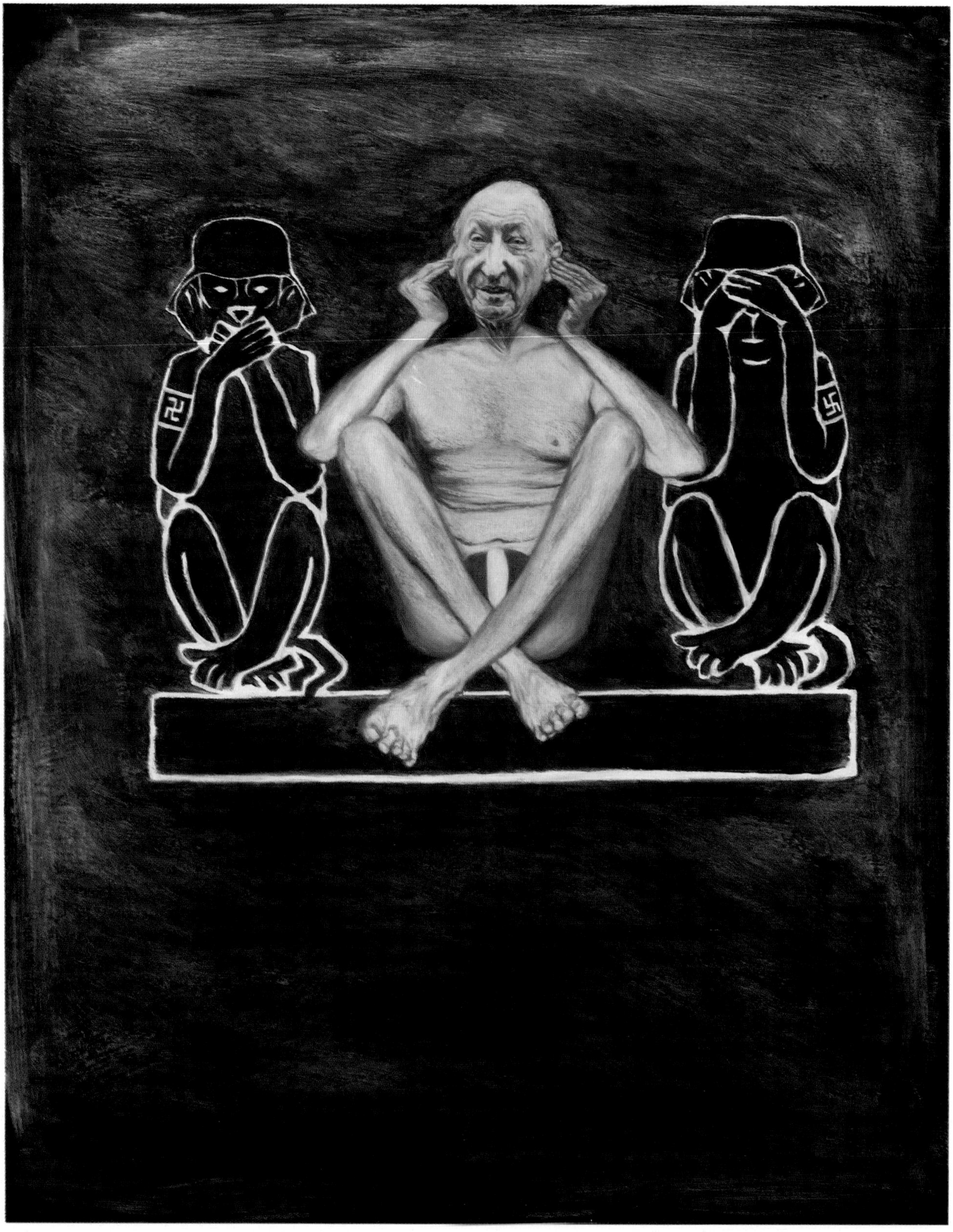

KURT WALDHEIM, PRESIDENT OF AUSTRIA

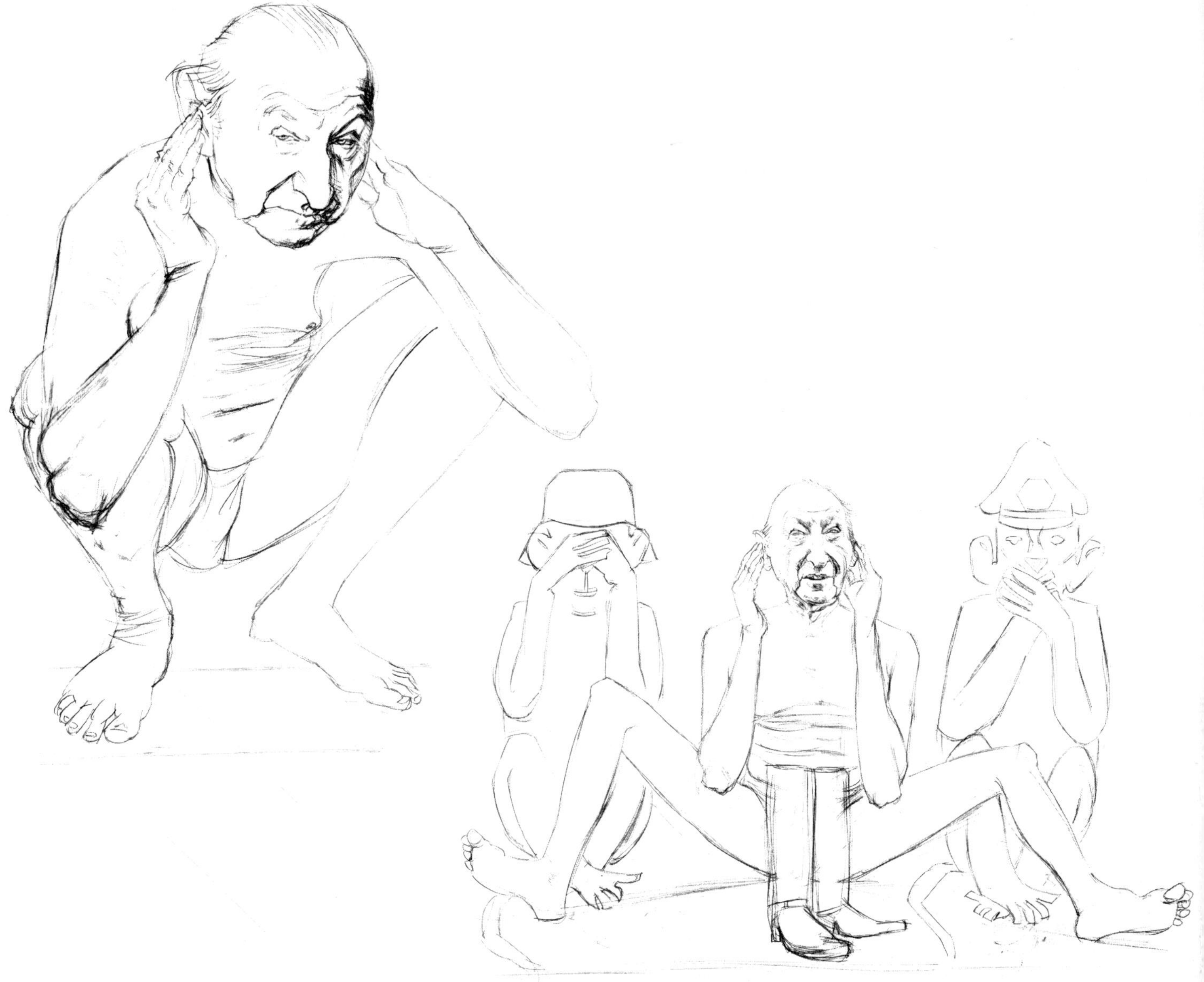

This poor little first lieutenant was accused of taking part in a partisan massacre, deporting Jews to concentration camps. Some say he was personally responsible for the murder of Jews. He says he was really nobody special.

Waldheim belongs to that group of bloody monkeys who don't talk, don't hear, don't see. But he is the only monkey who has taken power as the president of a Western democratic nation. Most of the others live in the jungles of South America.

Waldheim is living proof that sometimes politics happens to be real monkey business.

In the beginning I wanted to draw him naked with real monkeys. But then I moved to the more symbolic interpretation of the famous three monkeys from World War I.

I had a hard time doing this drawing because I had to keep myself from going too far with it. I think that the Nazi issue is beyond any kind of visual or symbolic imagination, and in this case I just wanted to point my finger at him, the new Austrian president.

MOVIES

KING KOCH

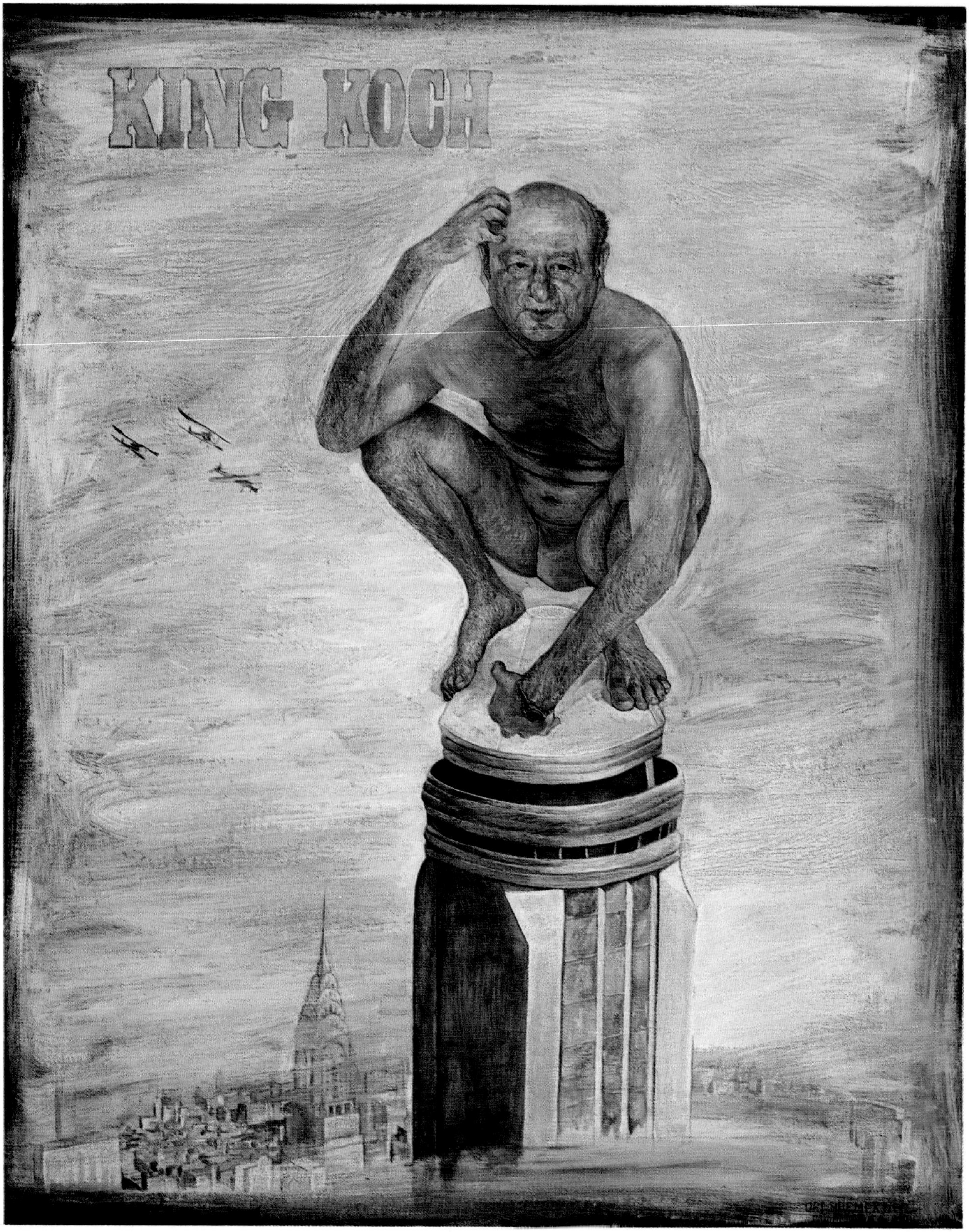
KING KOCH

ED KOCH, MAYOR OF NEW YORK CITY

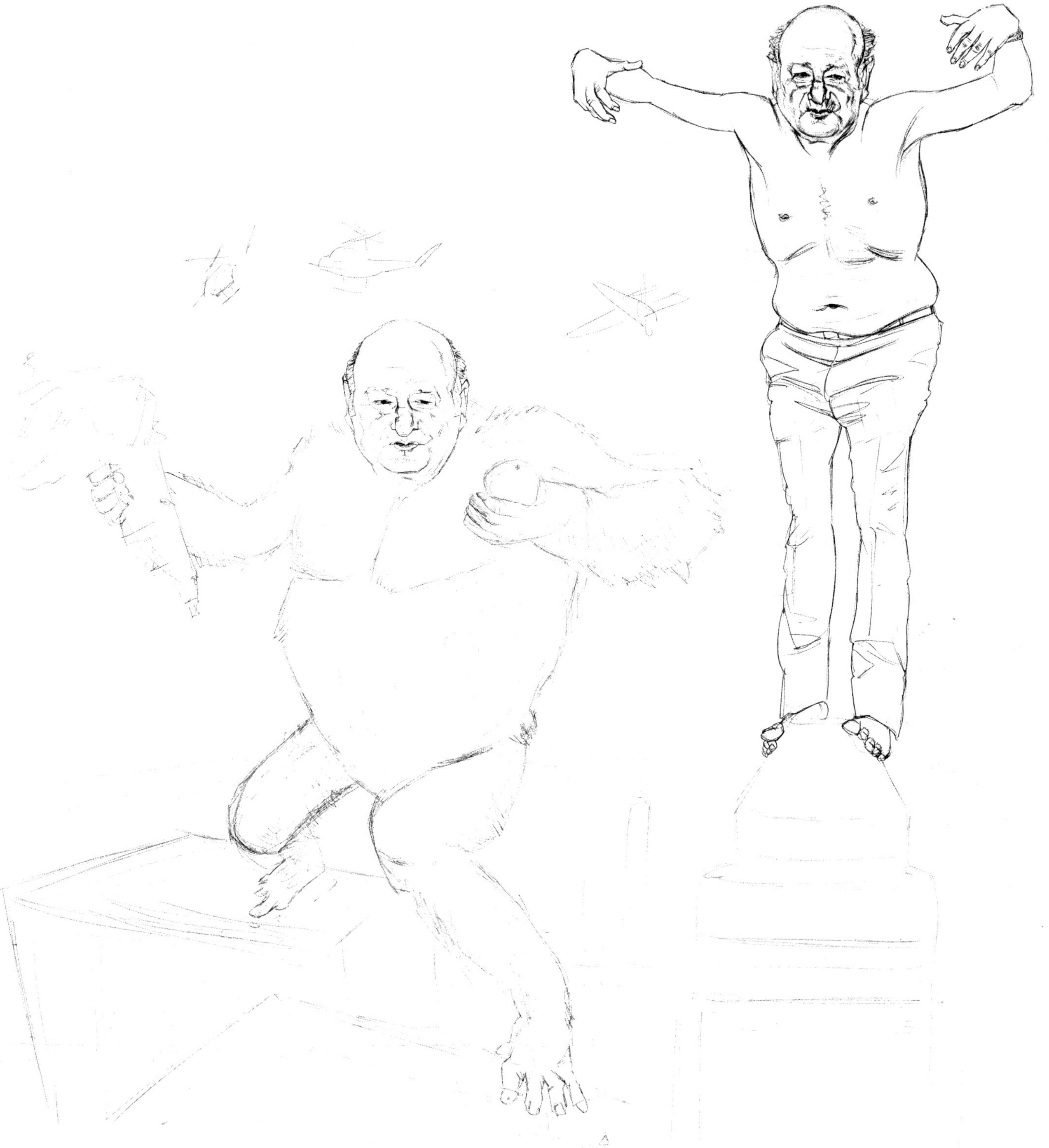

K*ing Kong* is a classic. Koch is a celebrity. In a few years he will be a classic as well.

This piece was done right before the 1985 mayoral election. It created enormous publicity. Koch said during the campaign that he wanted to use it as a publicity poster, and hang the original in City Hall.

At the time, it looked as if it would be more difficult to bring Koch down from the mayorship of New York than it would to take King Kong down from the Empire State Building.

NUCLEAR BALLS

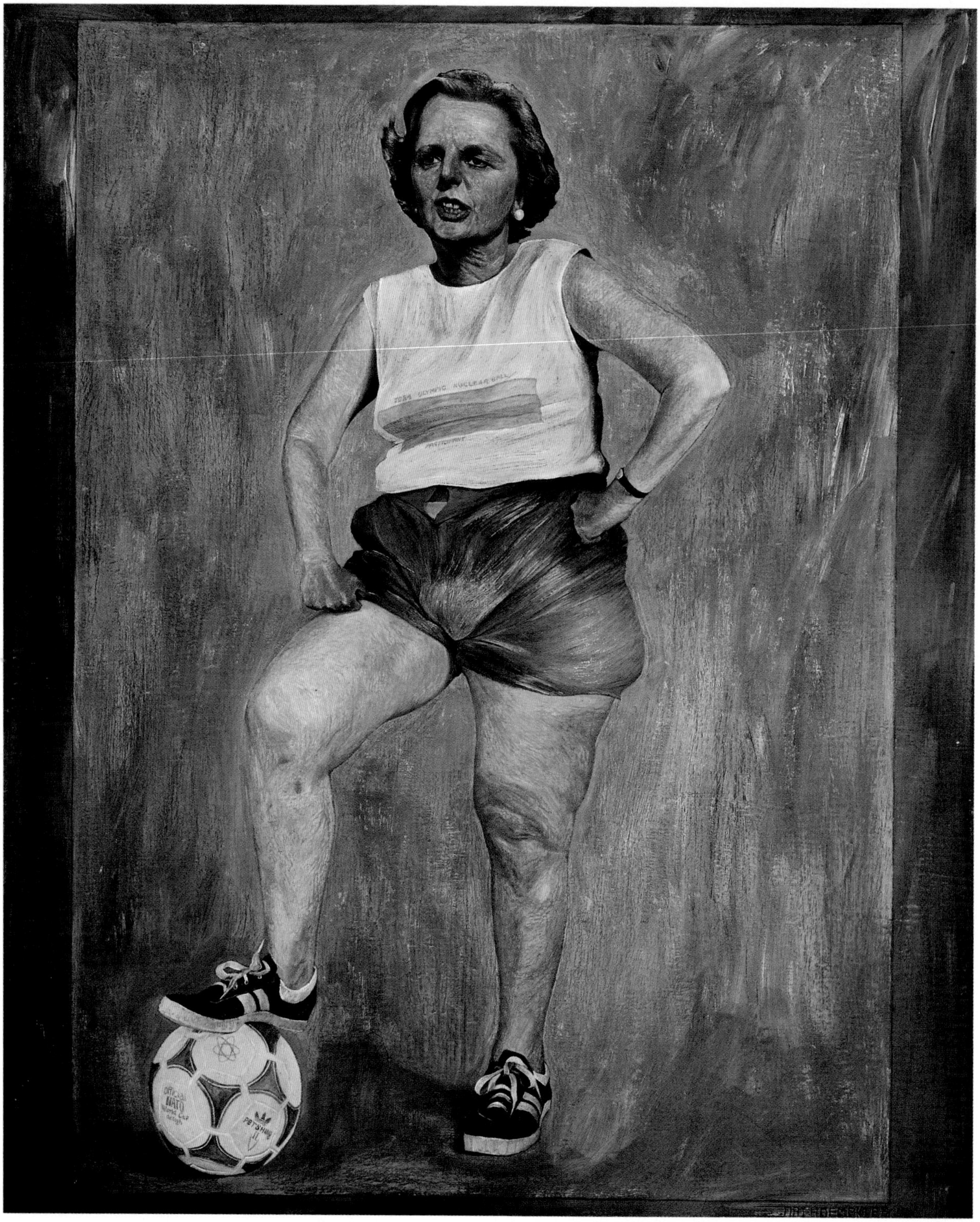
Official
NATO

MARGARET THATCHER,
PRIME MINISTER OF GREAT BRITAIN

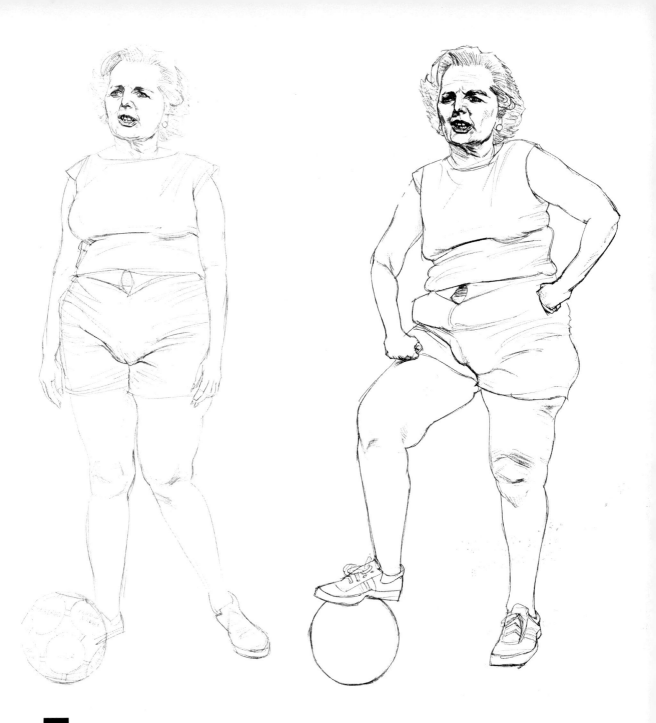

The major thing I can say about the old lady is that she is strong. She believes in power and she is a prime minister in a man's world. Thatcher is a thorough supporter of U.S. nuclear policy, which means nuclear missiles on Britain's soil.

During the 1984 Olympic Games, I wanted to contribute my own piece for the sport. The movie *Rollerball* gave me an inspiration for a kind of combination of power and sports and politics. That was exactly what I needed in order to finish my sportive idea for Maggie. On the ball I put nuclear signs instead of a trademark.

In order to get Maggie's legs right, I had to use my own model. It wasn't easy to get a lady to jump with bare legs and play with a ball in all these poses. But I needed an idea of how Thatcher would look if she were asked to play a nuclear ball game in my studio.

JIMMY HORROR PICTURE SHOW

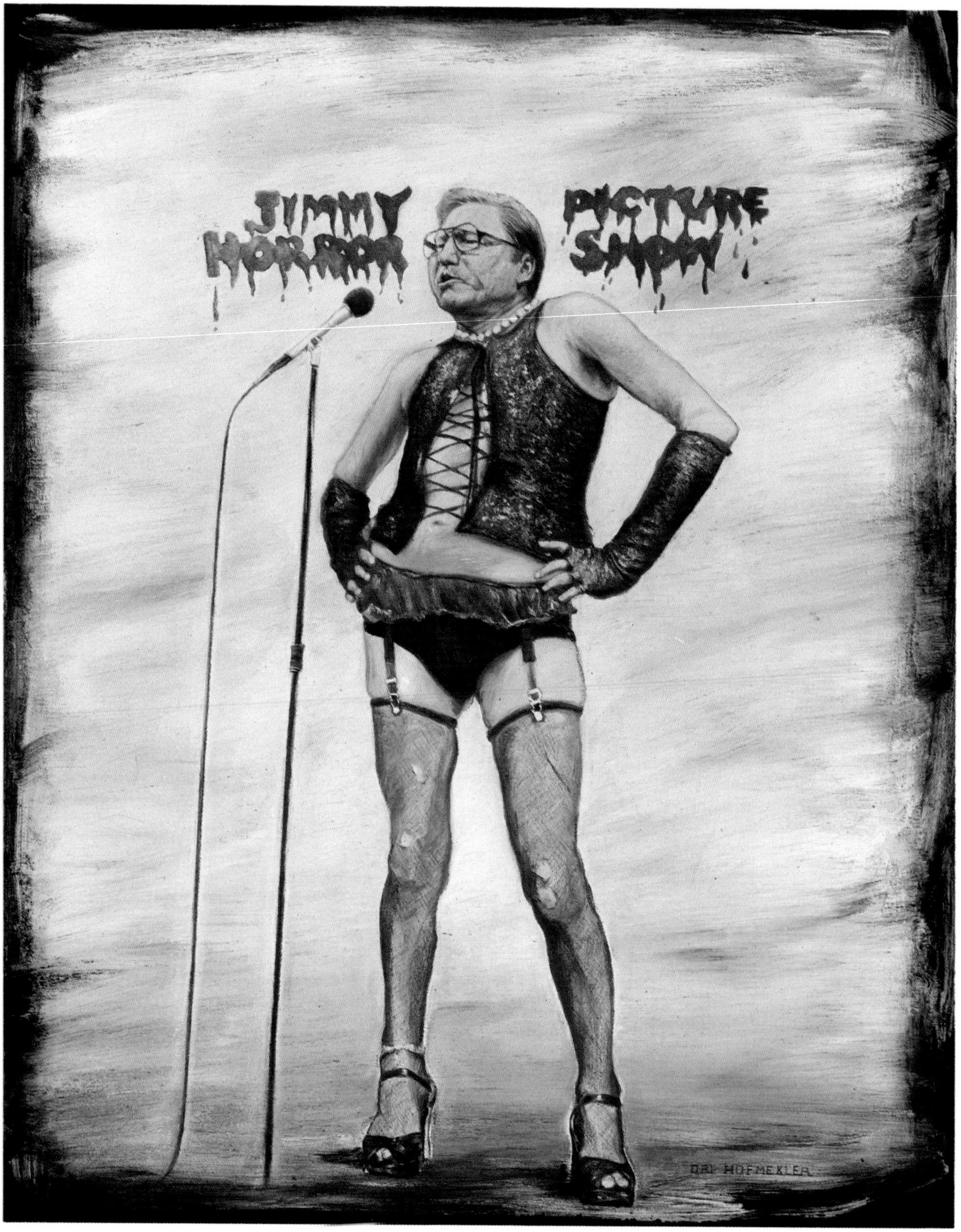
JIMMY HORROR
PICTURE SHOW
ORI HOFMEKLER

JIMMY SWAGGART, TV EVANGELIST

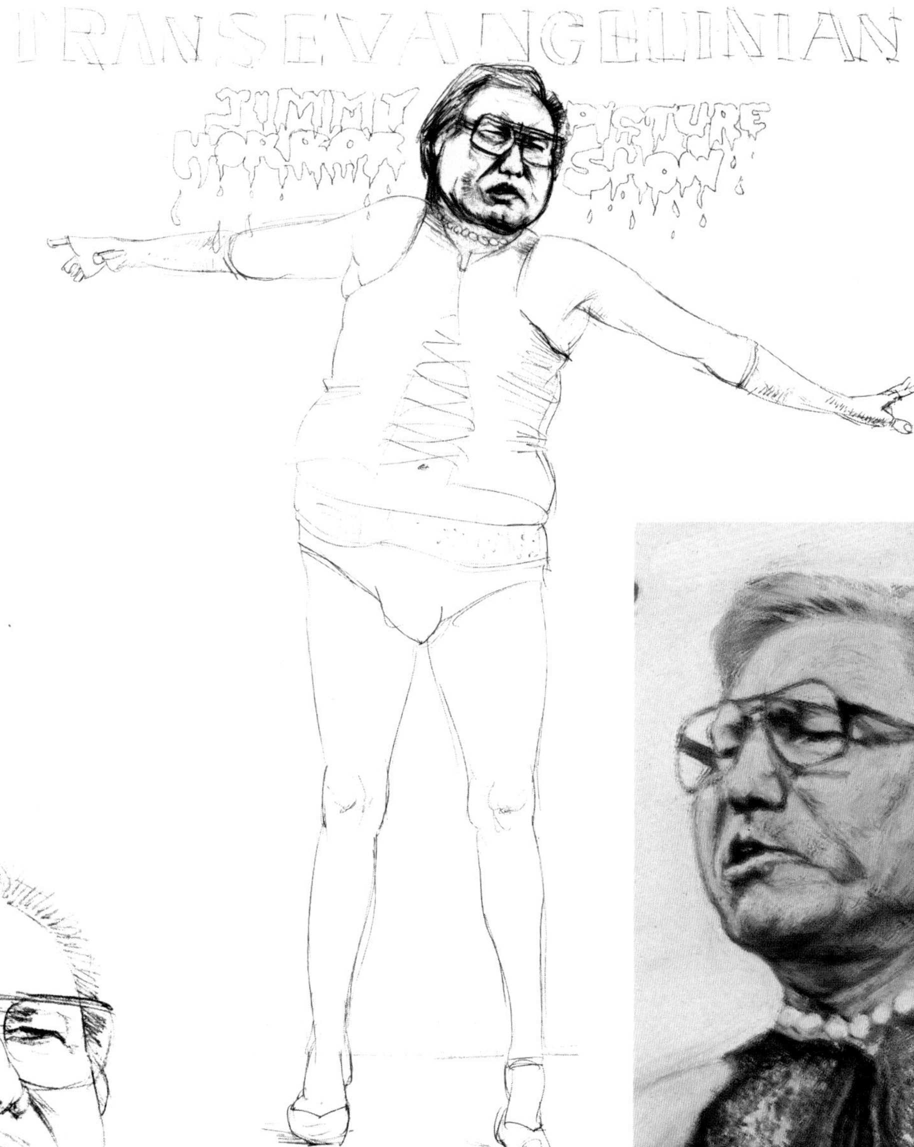
TRANSEVANGELINIAN
JIMMY HORROR
PICTURE SHOW

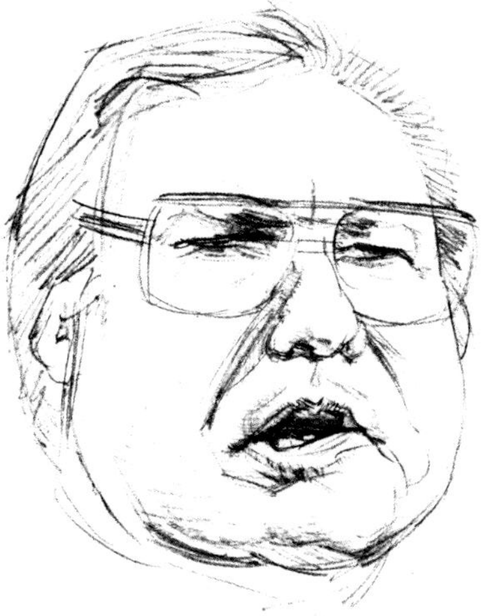

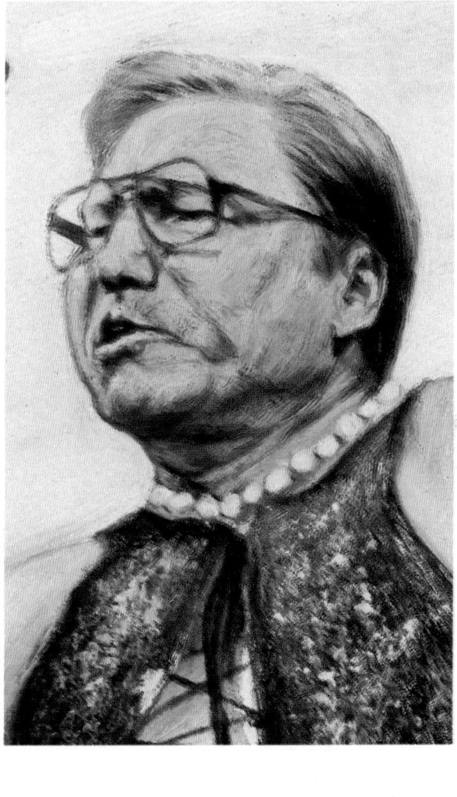

I've never been bored by a Jimmy Swaggart show. There is always the excitement of the good guys fighting the bad guys. The good guys are those who believe in Swaggart's Christ; all the rest are possessed by the devil, without whom there would be no show. Swaggart has a Devil Complex. Talking so much about evil and the devil and the other world makes his show look like a horror film.

The theme is that the Russians and rock musicians are planning to destroy the world, and Jimmy is trying to save the planet. In my show, Mr. Swaggart takes the role of Mr. Frank N. Furter from *The Rocky Horror Picture Show.* Jimmy likes to perform and to demonstrate his philosophy. I gave him a chance for once to show us what obscenity looks like.

BOB & CAROL & TED & ALICE

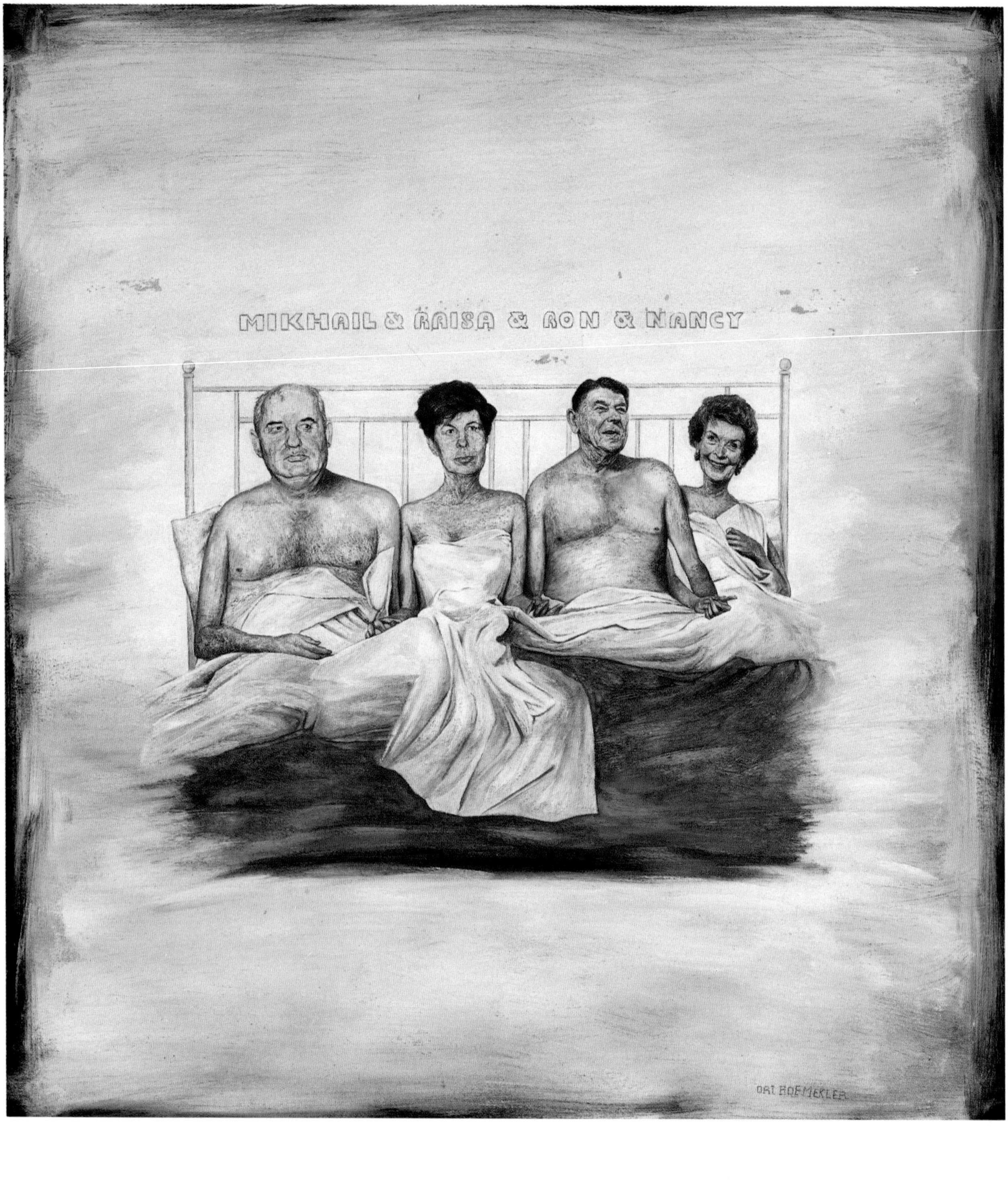
MIKHAIL & RAISA & RON & NANCY
DRT HOFMEKLER

MIKHAIL & RAISA & RON & NANCY

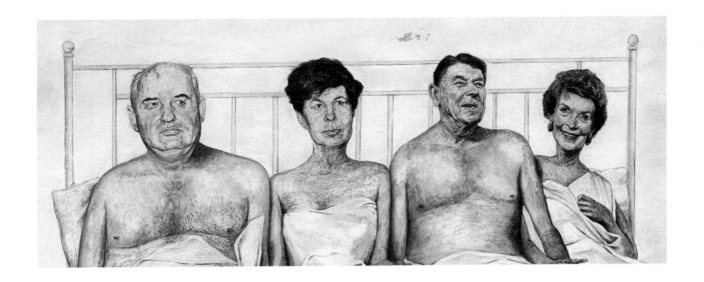

This picture is my contribution to peace. It looks to me to be a perfect alternative to a Russian/American summit. There are so many summits already and nothing really happens besides long talks. I think that the leaders and their wives should share a bed and see whether it works or not in reality.

I've tried to make the scene look like it would in the movie, and to keep the characters as they are. Gorbachev stays cool. He tries to control himself. He is suspicious.

Raisa is frozen between her husband and Reagan. She tries to show sympathy.

Ron is smiling. That's because he's always smiling.

Nancy is cheerful because she knows that the world is watching her. Or because she likes to smile when Reagan is smiling.

I have to admit that I don't believe my suggestion is going to work, but there's nothing to lose.

MAN IN RED

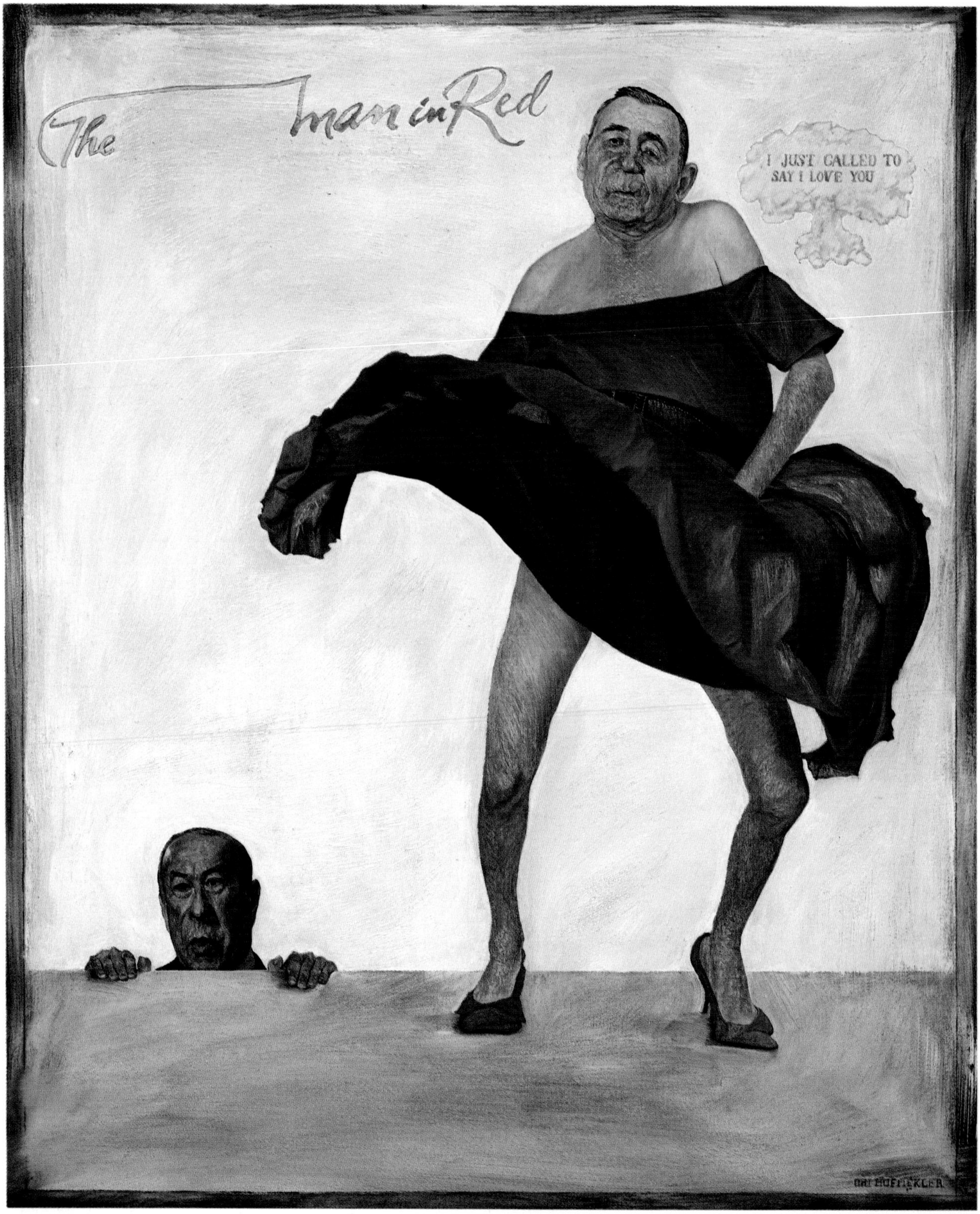
The Man in Red
I JUST CALLED TO
SAY I LOVE YOU

ANDREY GROMYKO,
PRESIDENT OF THE U.S.S.R.

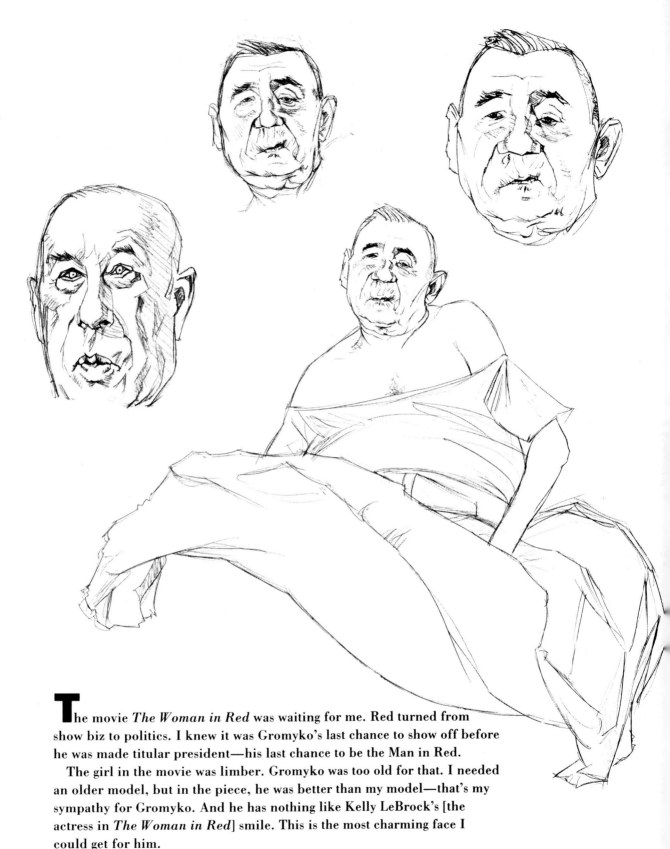

The movie *The Woman in Red* was waiting for me. Red turned from
show biz to politics. I knew it was Gromyko's last chance to show off before
he was made titular president—his last chance to be the Man in Red.

    The girl in the movie was limber. Gromyko was too old for that. I needed
an older model, but in the piece, he was better than my model—that's my
sympathy for Gromyko. And he has nothing like Kelly LeBrock's [the
actress in *The Woman in Red*] smile. This is the most charming face I
could get for him.

    From a Western point of view, the search for peace is like the Woman in
Red. She's beautiful, but she's an illusion, like the summit. Just as I'm
suspicious about my ability to get the ideal woman, I'm also suspicious
about our chances for peace.

HEAVEN CAN WAIT

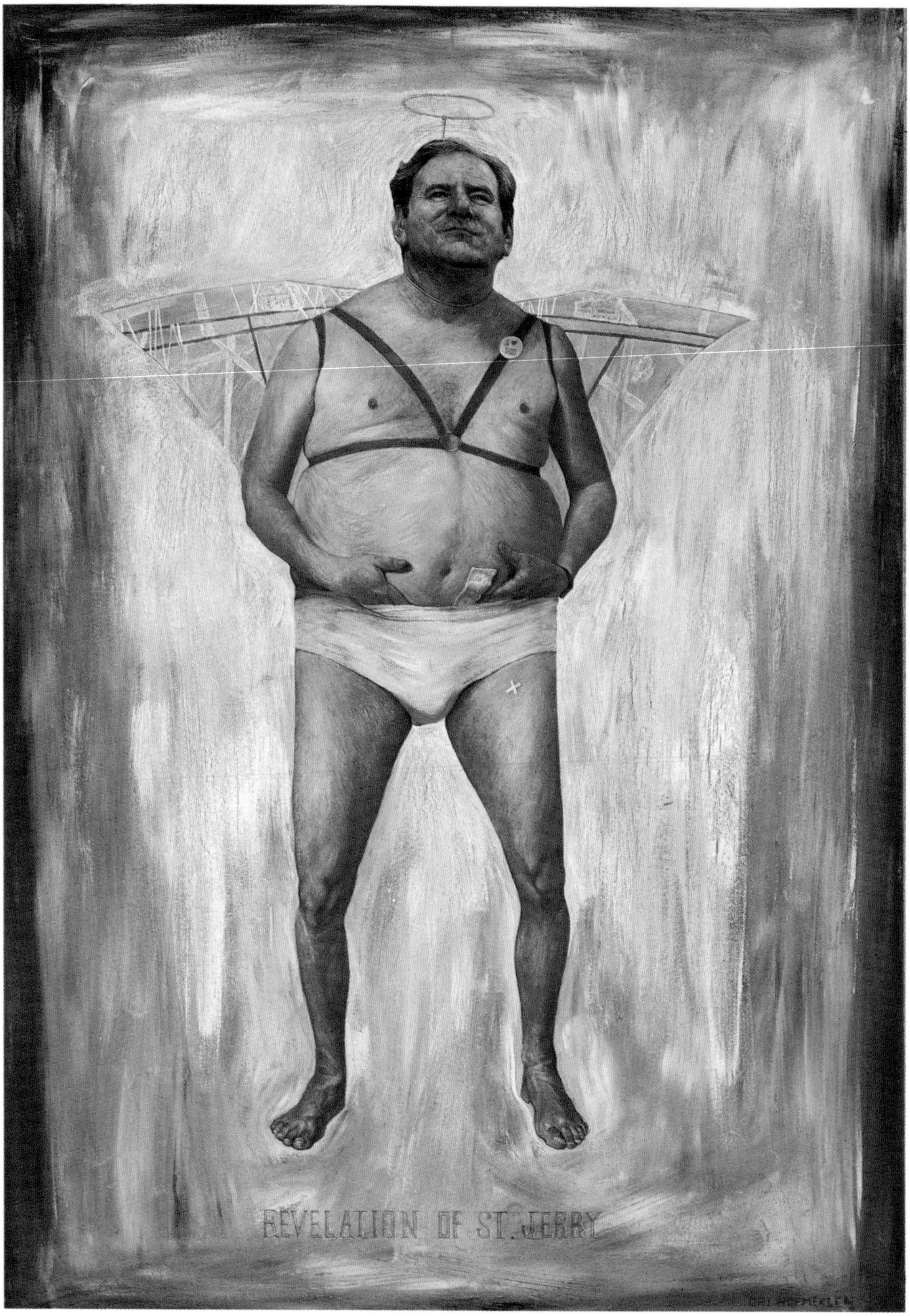

REVELATION OF ST. JERRY

REVEREND JERRY FALWELL,
LEADER OF THE MORAL MAJORITY

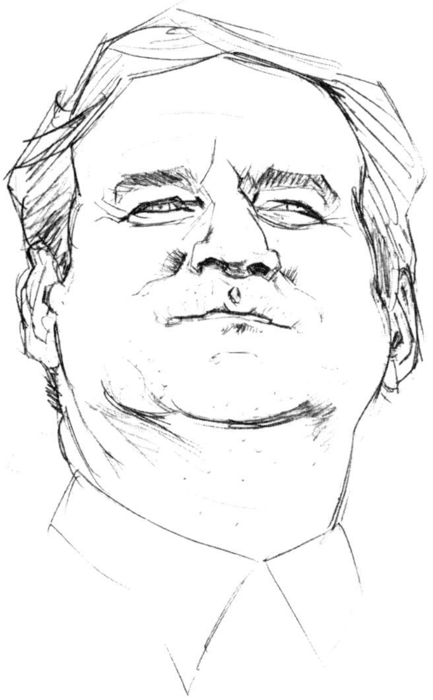

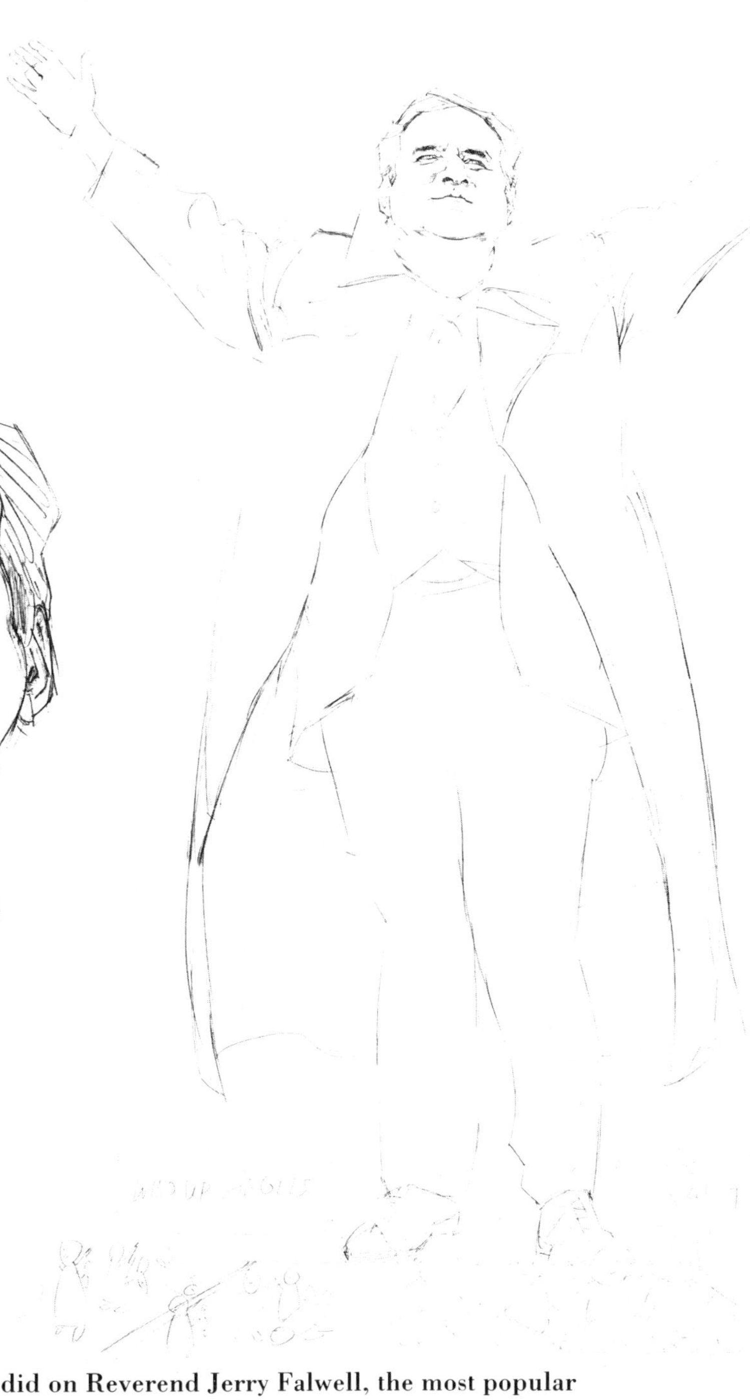

This is the first piece I did on Reverend Jerry Falwell, the most popular and powerful preacher among the televangelists.

My first idea was to paint him as a flim-flam, someone who sells cheap things on the corner of the street. *Penthouse* publisher Bob Guccione had the idea to put some plastic angels—toys—on the suitcase, for sale. I liked this idea, and tried to envision Cabbage Patch angels. Then I thought of Falwell as Crazy Eddie, whose exuberant arm-waving, ranting commercials have helped him sell millions of dollars worth of audio equipment.

But then one evening I saw in a photographic magazine a picture of a naked girl trying to look like an angel, with some kind of feathered wings tied to her shoulders. It reminded me of the movie *Heaven Can Wait*.

Here he tries to look like an angel, complete with handmade wings. Angels are not always naked, but cupids are. And following a great tradition, he is still wearing his shorts.

BALLBUSTERS

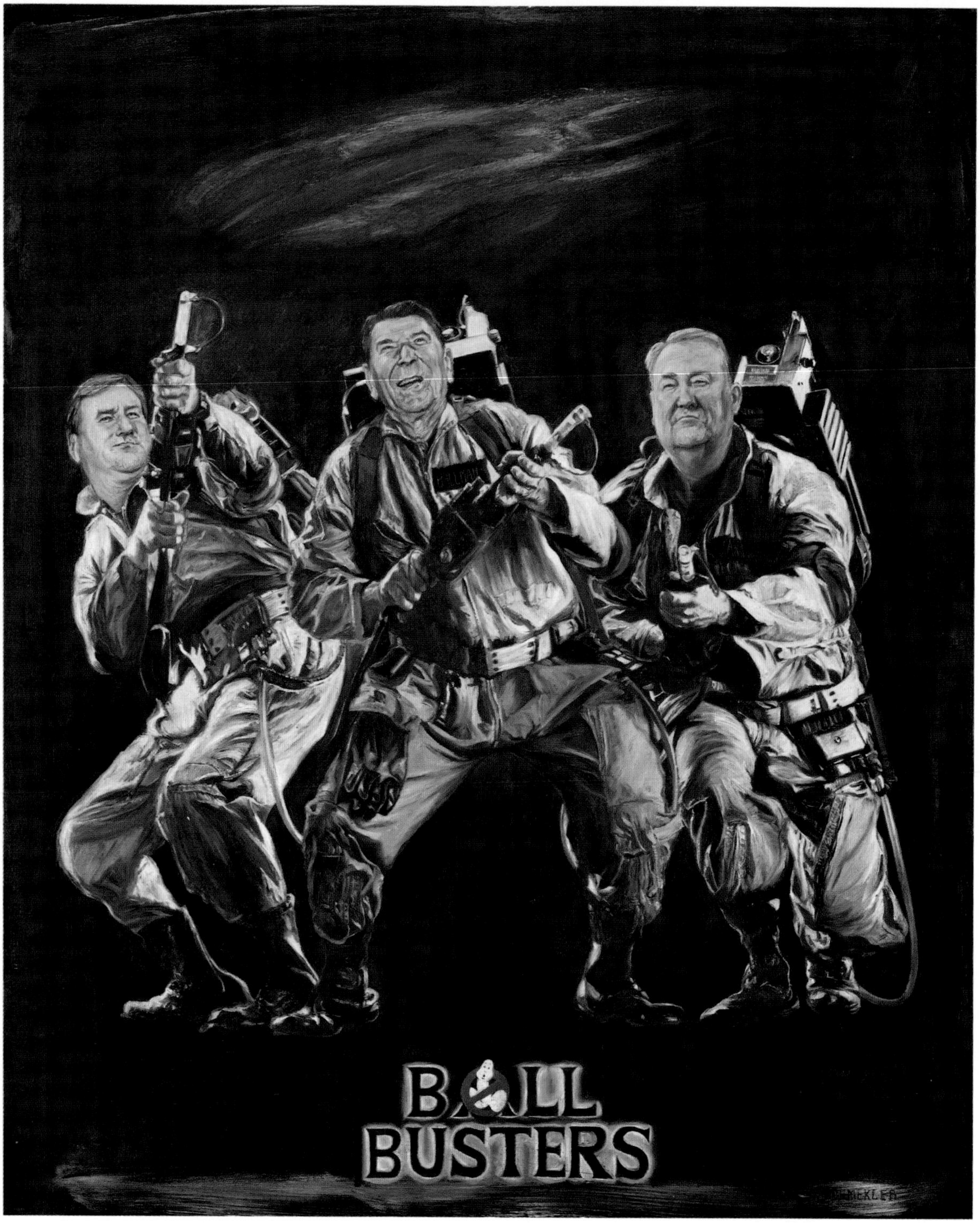
BALL
BUSTERS

EDWIN MEESE, U.S. ATTORNEY GENERAL,
RONALD REAGAN, PRESIDENT OF THE UNITED STATES,
REVEREND JERRY FALWELL, LEADER
OF THE MORAL MAJORITY

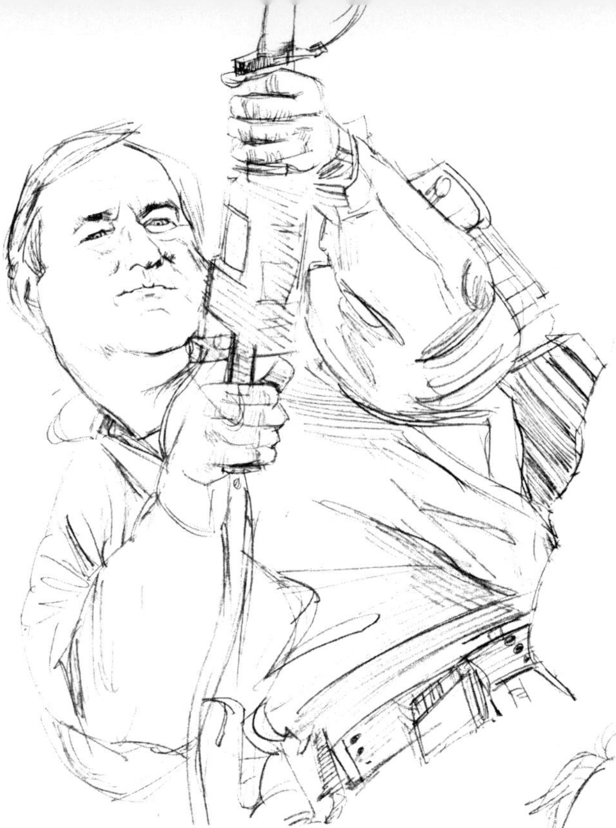

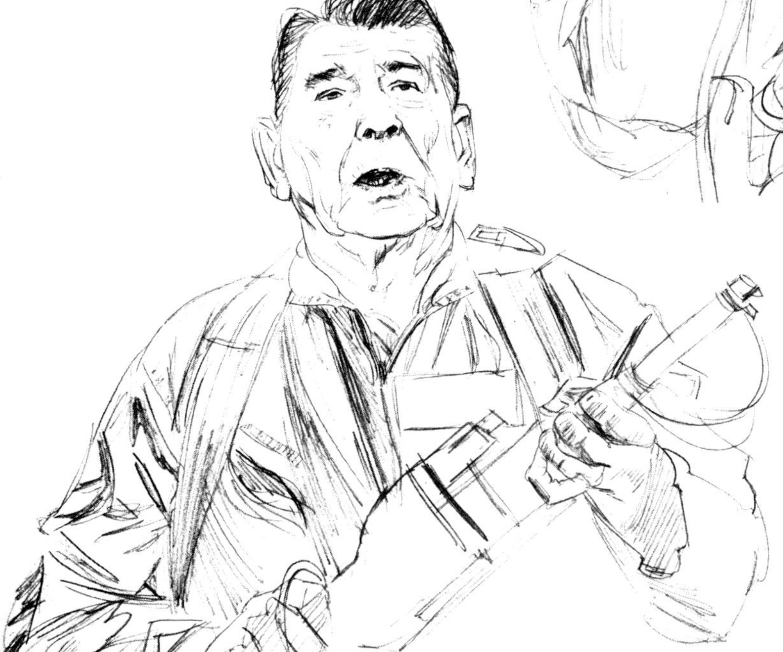

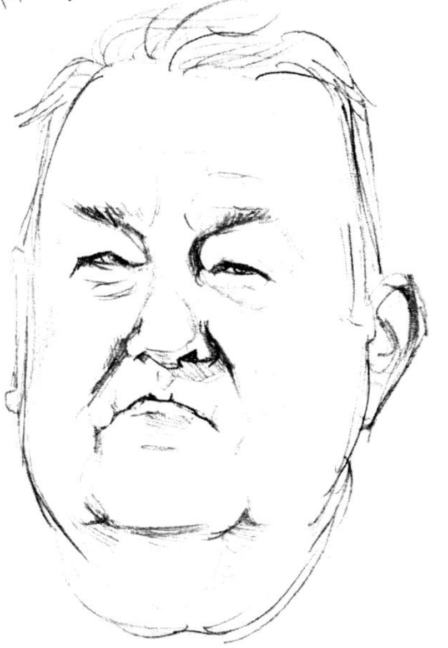

For a couple of days I had been stumped by the subject of censorship and obscenity, which from time to time is pushed beyond all proportion in America. I tried a lot of ideas, but nothing was strong enough. Then one day, after seeing *Ghostbusters* on cable TV, I found myself sketching a new idea at four o'clock in the morning. I knew I had it, though I changed my technique to get a more spontaneous and open drawing.

Behind any kind of censorship there is a philosophy. It is always a kitschy philosophy because of its sterile world view, making life all good or all bad and taking out the freedom to choose. Behind any kitsch stands an establishment, whether it is religious or political. Religious leaders talk about "paradise" and political leaders talk about "the new spirit of America" or wherever. Both are talking kitsch.

Trying to understand what the issue is all about, perhaps Reagan, Falwell, and Meese face a traumatic experience when they take off their pants. Maybe they try to censor anything that reminds them of the problem.

HEROES

RAMBO

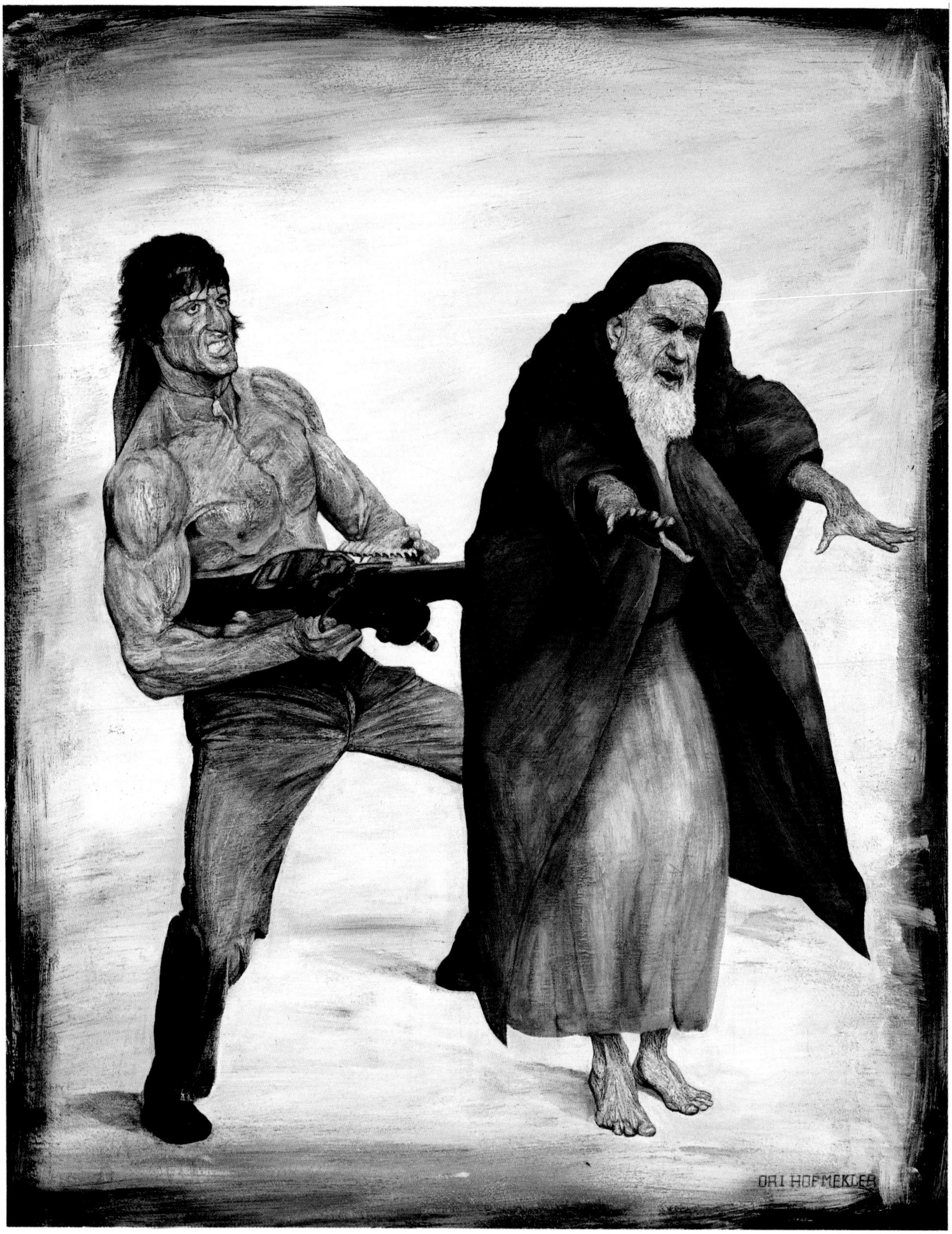
ORI HOFMEKLER

THE AYATOLLAH KHOMEINI

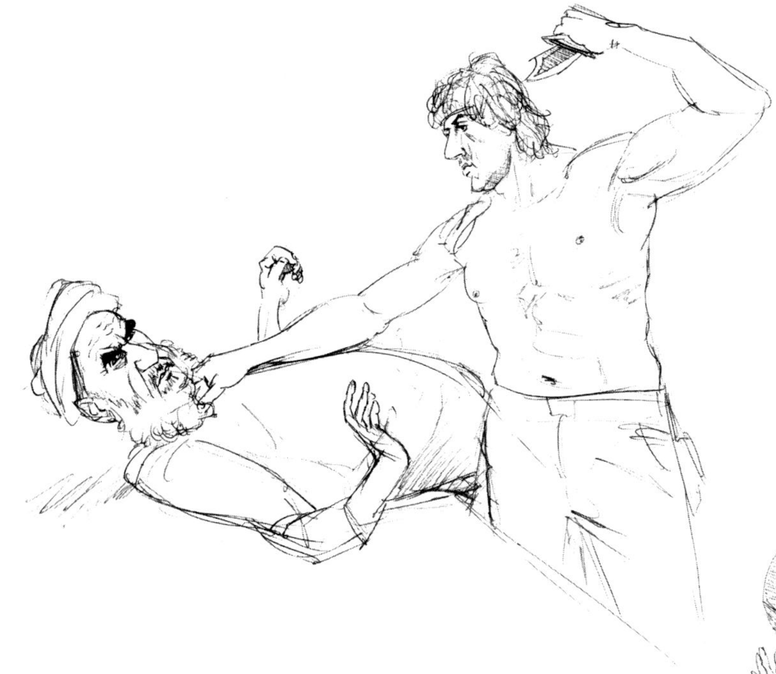

MISSION COMPLETED

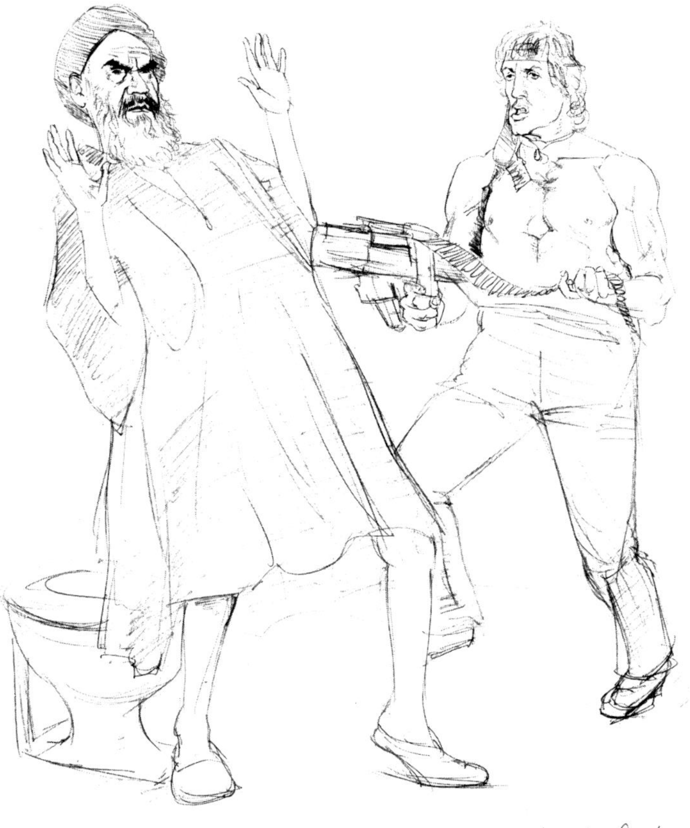

ON YOUR Feet Motherfucker

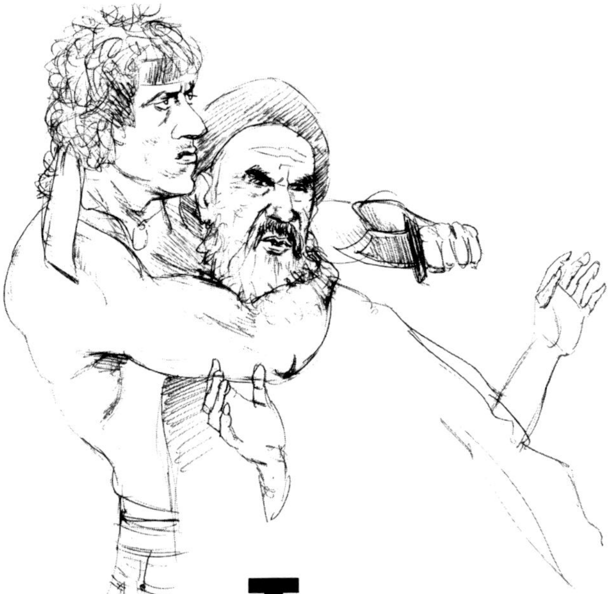

The Americans were defeated in Vietnam. They lost their case in Lebanon. They were victimized by Khomeini. The "American dream" isn't holding up, and now there is a desire for revenge.

Revenge is a primitive desire which, if you use it right, works and sells just like sex. Stallone understands this, and that's where Rambo comes in. In politics and show biz, there is one rule: if you want to make a hit, you had better give people what they want. In this case, revenge.

The revenge theme has worked so well that Stallone was invited to the Republican Convention as a guest of honor by President Reagan. That's because Reagan thinks that Rambo definitely solved the Vietnam problem.

Now the Iranian case still bothers America. Khomeini is the one who drew first blood. Here Rambo is going to get him good for Reagan.

COMMANDO

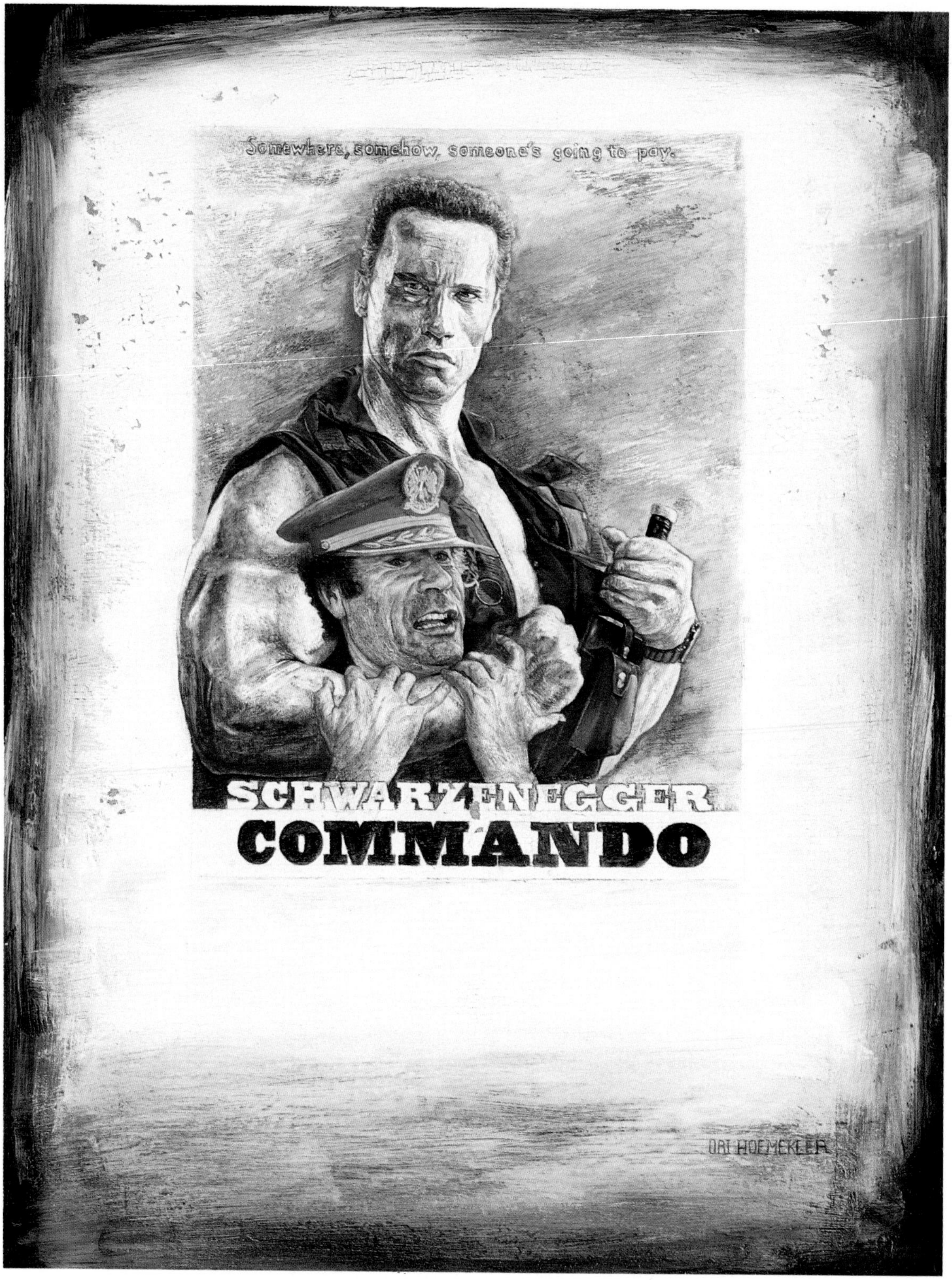
Somewhere, somehow, someone's going to pay.
SCHWARZENEGGER
COMMANDO
ORI HOFMEKLER

ARNOLD SCHWARZENEGGER, MOVIE STAR,
AND MUAMMAR QADDAFI, PRESIDENT OF LIBYA

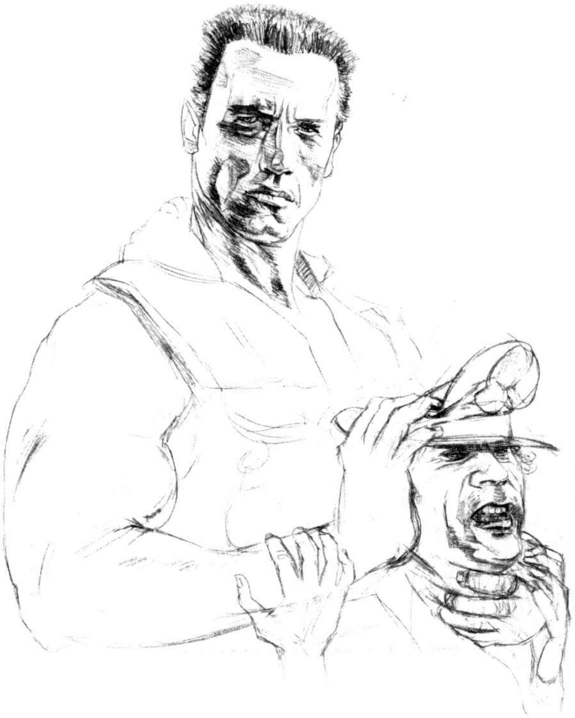

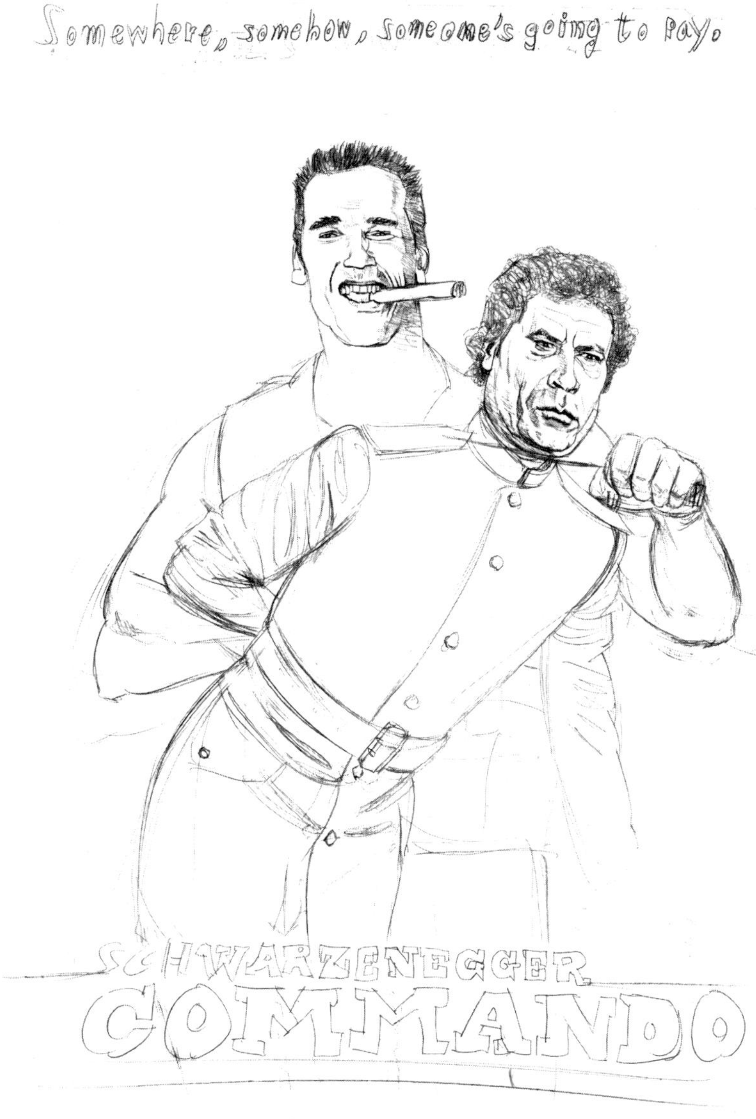
Somewhere, somehow, someone's going to pay.
SCHWARZENEGGER
COMMANDO

The second worst man in the world after Khomeini is Muammar Qaddafi. The second toughest guy in the world after Rambo is Arnold Schwarzenegger. Since Rambo has already solved the Vietnam problem and since I already sent him to get Khomeini in my *Rambo* piece, there is only Schwarzenegger to get Qaddafi.

Commando is another example of kitsch: simplistic definitions of good and bad, nothing with a question mark, and always a happy ending (no anti-heroes here!).

Maybe Arnold is right, we must use muscle to finish something. Now that I've finished *Commando*, Arnold should be President Reagan's guest of honor.

When I drew Qaddafi in this piece, I had no problem with his face. He always looks so crazy; with his expression, he could be transported without alteration to sit under the arm of Schwarzenegger. He always looks like someone just cornered him, like a beast trying to get out of a trap.

RONNY II

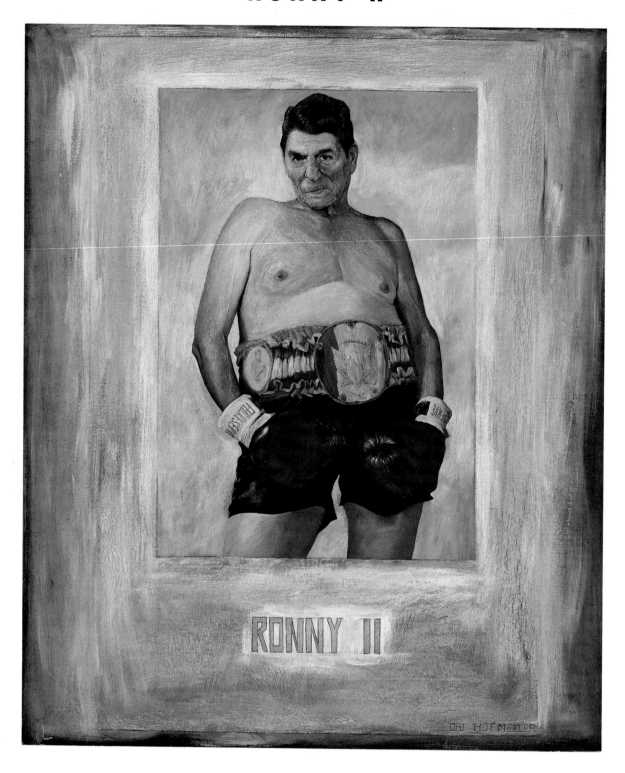

RONALD REAGAN, PRESIDENT OF THE UNITED STATES

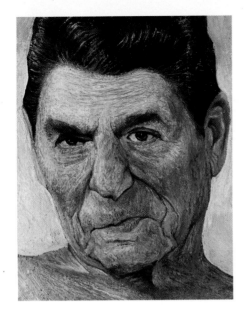

This piece was done just before the 1984 presidential election. *Rocky II* put Stallone's image deep in the American consciousness. Moreover, the poster of that movie was the strongest visual still of all the *Rocky* movies. Stallone was standing like a hero, showing his muscles and his champion's belt.

I got the feeling that Reagan was going to win the election. I didn't need much more of a reason than that to put him in the poster. I tried to keep the Stallone-Rocky expression on Reagan's face and to retain his fluffy body.

I was very lucky with this piece. It was published as a poster and distributed all over the country. It was publicized in the newspapers and on TV. Even President Reagan sent a letter of gratitude to the poster publisher.

But in spite of the fact that Ronny was a winner and everybody loved it, inside I felt sorry. I had wanted to illustrate another power play of Reagan's. But when you are facetious or ironic, sometimes you risk having people misunderstand you.

TARZAN

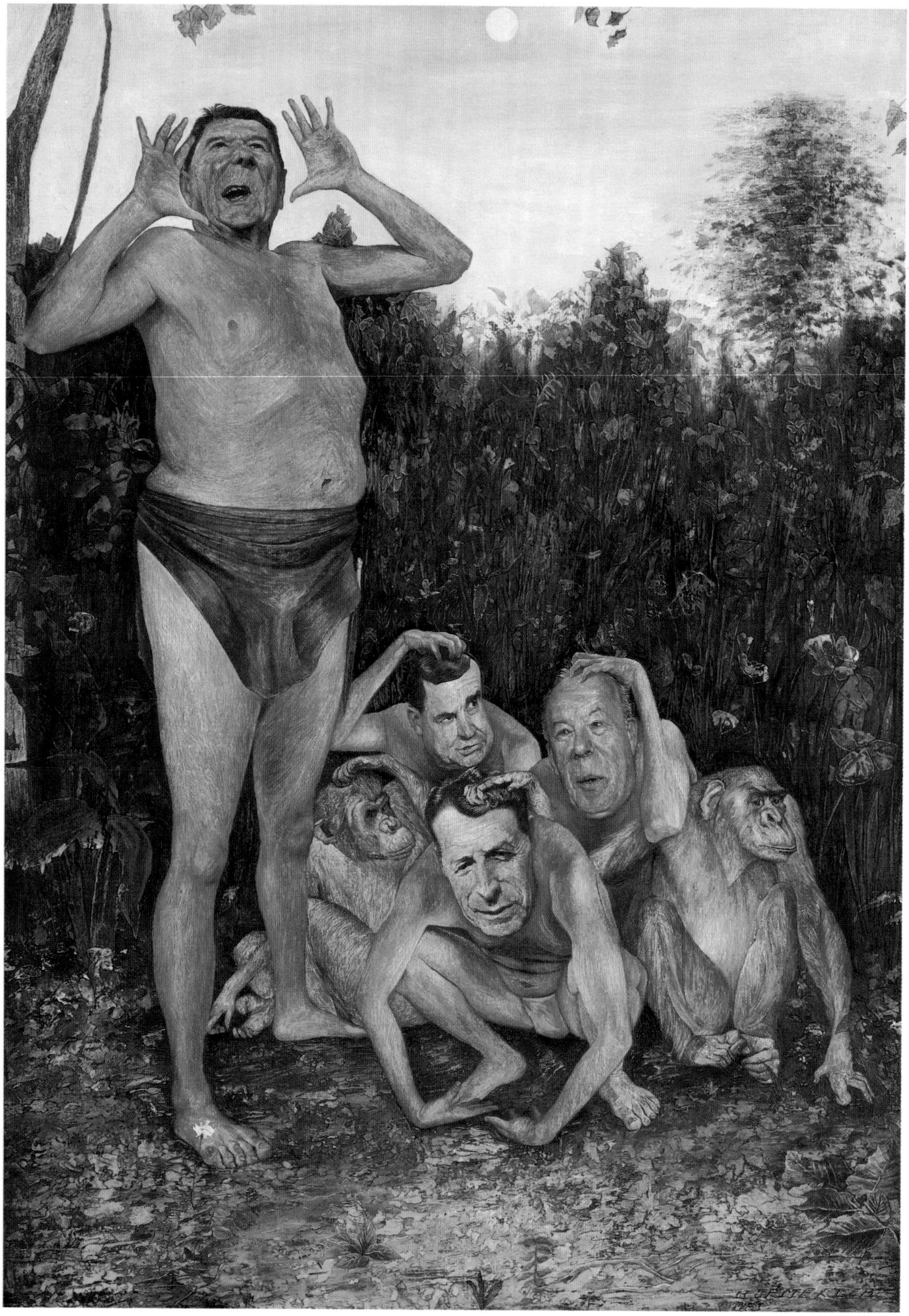

RONALD REAGAN, PRESIDENT OF THE UNITED STATES

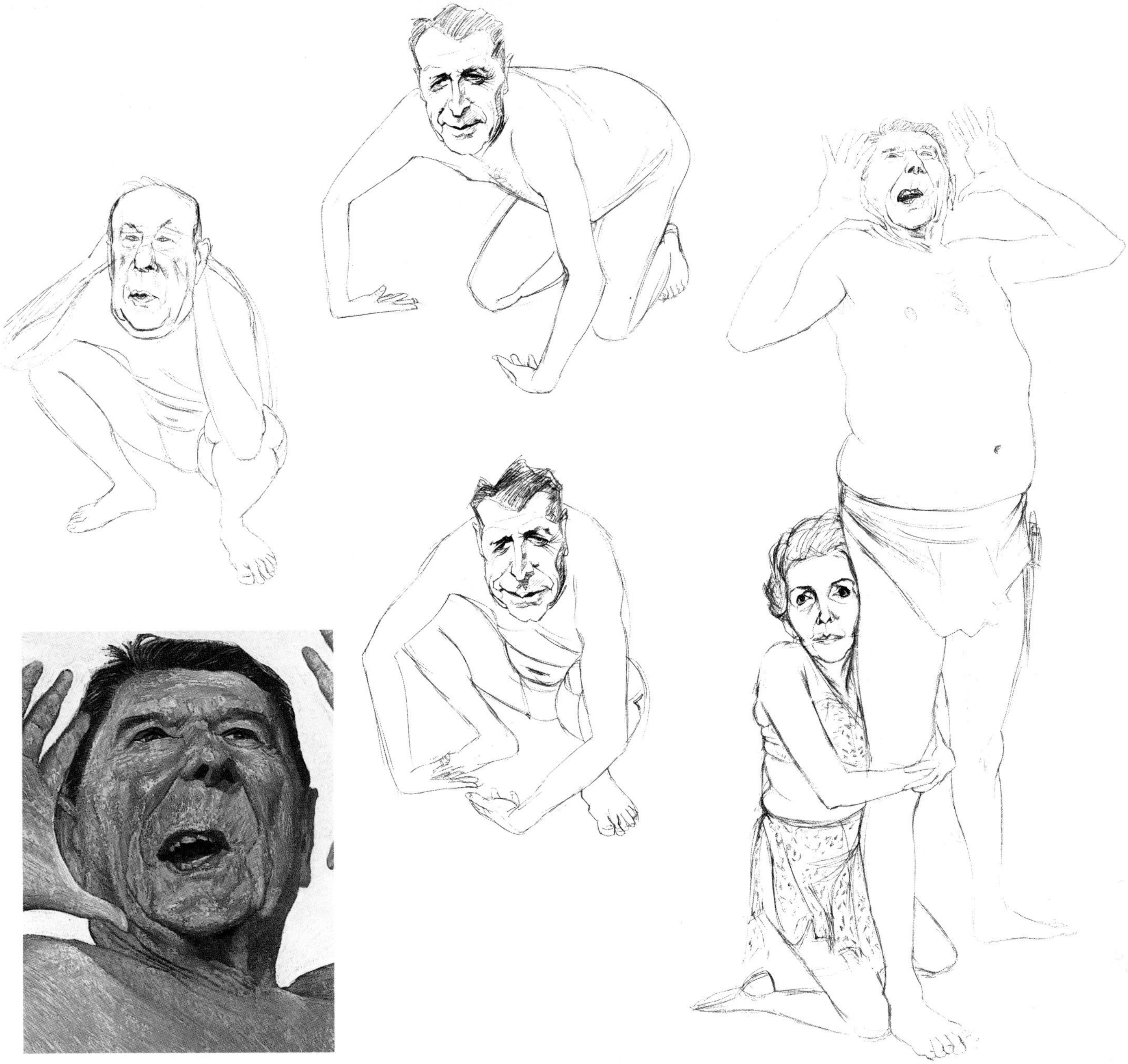

This piece was done at the time of the TV movie *The Day After*, about a nuclear disaster. I saw it as *A Day After—Back to the Jungle.* It was a nice chance to portray the president and his top aides in the wilderness. My son Daniel asked me again and again to draw him a Tarzan and monkeys. I drew him two real chimpanzees, but it didn't satisfy him. "This is not Tarzan. Why did you draw this fluffy guy again? This is Chaplin, not Tarzan." (He calls Reagan "Chaplin" because of the Reagan-Chaplin picture that you've already seen, which was actually the first piece I did on Reagan.) I guess my son was right. But I can't help it; I was thinking of *The Day After*, the world was in effect being reinvented.

In my scene I've tried to keep the relationship between Reagan and his aides. Instead of sitting in the Oval Room discussing monkey business, they're here in the jungle discussing world business affairs. The only ones who feel embarrassed in this scene are the two real chimpanzees.